DAILY STRENGTH
FOR MEN

365 DEVOTIONS

BroadStreet
PUBLISHING

BroadStreet Publishing Group, LLC.
Savage, Minnesota, USA
Broadstreetpublishing.com

Daily Strength for Men (Daily Promises)
© 2023 by BroadStreet Publishing®

9781424567690

Typesetting and design by Garborg Design Works | garborgdesign.com
Compiled by Michelle Winger | literallyprecise.com. Edited by Carole Holdahl.

Printed in China.

23 24 25 26 27 28 29 7 6 5 4 3 2 1

THE OFF SWITCH

> "Six days you shall labor and do all your work,
> but the seventh day is a sabbath to the LORD your God.
> On it you shall not do any work."
> EXODUS 20:9-10 NIV

God gave the Israelites a mandatory off switch called the Sabbath. On this day they stopped working to honor God. When you have a rhythm of rest and work, it helps keep you from burning out. Take some time to rest today and do something that honors God, so you can be filled up.

How can you honor God in your rest?

GOD IS NEAR

The LORD is near to all who call on him,
to all who call on him in truth.

PSALM 145:18 NIV

God is near when you call him. He never lets your call go to voicemail. He has time for you, and it's his heart's desire to spend that time—anytime—with you. Sometimes your perception of him may be skewed because of your own sin. You may think he's not listening or busy with others, but that is not true. God is always near. Reflect on that as you consider the year you have walked through and the new year ahead.

Do you know that God is always near when you call on him?

YOUR CROSS

"Whoever wants to be my disciple must deny themselves
and take up their cross and follow me."
MATTHEW 16:24 NIV

Following Jesus brings joy, but it is also a big sacrifice. The word *sacrifice* may make you think of a missionary or someone who donates a lot of money. That is sometimes what God calls you to do, but sacrifice also means helping a sick friend in the night, volunteering at a soup kitchen, or praying with a co-worker. These are the little sacrifices that reap the greatest rewards.

How can you sacrifice your time and energy to serve God?

GENUINE INTERACTION

How delightfully good
when brothers live together in harmony!
PSALM 133:1 CSB

If your life is filled with texts, email, and social posting, it makes it easy to overlook the fact that you haven't actually seen your friends in a while. The psalmist wrote that it's important to spend meaningful time together. True relationships are nurtured through engaging in genuine interaction, where deep connections and accountability flourish. Living with others in unity is truly beneficial.

Are you intentionally living in God's presence with others?

AFFIRMATION

Jacob took the food to his father. "My father?" he said.
"Yes, my son," Isaac answered. "Who are you—Esau or Jacob?"
GENESIS 27:18 NLT

Isaac preferred his older son, Esau, an outdoorsman. Jacob stayed home and cooked. Near the end of Isaac's life, Jacob dressed like Esau and deceived his father. Even though this situation seems farfetched, it is common. You may live without any affirmation of love. Remember that God gave his Son so you may feel his love and be called his kid. That love heals affirmation vacancies and provides an example of how you can love others.

How can you love like God does?

SHARING THE STORY

"You will receive power when the Holy Spirit has come upon you, and you will be my witnesses in Jerusalem and in all Judea and Samaria, and to the end of the earth."

ACTS 1:8 ESV

The magnificent Creator and Sustainer of the universe has entrusted you with the responsibility of sharing his story with the world. His purpose involves you spreading his message wherever you are now and wherever you will go. You are not alone in this effort; you have the Holy Spirit as your guide and the source of power to accomplish this eternal task.

Do you rely on the Holy Spirit to lead you in sharing the story of Jesus?

OUR FATHER

"This, then, is how you should pray:
'Our Father....'"
MATTHEW 6:9 NIV

Throughout the Bible are many titles for God. In the New Testament when Jesus is teaching his followers to pray, he calls God, "our Father." Imagine. The infinite, sovereign, Creator wants you to know him as *Dad*. And Jesus speaks about God as a Father who scans the horizon looking for his lost children, and then he runs to them. God is a Father whose love is intimate and protective.

How can you know your sovereign God as your kind Father?

FAITH

"Lord, to whom will we go?
You have the words of eternal life."
JOHN 6:68 CSB

Simon Peter wasn't known for being cautious about speaking, and he often stumbled over his words. But in today's verse he uttered something worth repeating. When Jesus was abandoned by many of his followers, he asked his closest disciples if they too would leave. Peter's confession of faith has echoed throughout time. The Words of Christ bring everlasting life. There is nowhere else to go.

Are you in agreement with Peter?

HALLOWED BE

"Hallowed be your name."
MATTHEW 6:9 NIV

Holy may make you think "moral" or "religious," but those definitions miss the biblical meaning. God is perfect and all-powerful. Jesus says you should call God "Father," but also understand he is holy. God is beyond and near, powerful and meek, warrior and loving. In the Lord's Prayer, Jesus invited you into the beautiful mystery of God's full identity. Reflecting on this may blow you away. Then you're on the right track.

Are you close enough to God to be amazed?

POINTING OUT JESUS

John, gazing upon Jesus, pointed to him and prophesied,
"Look! There's God's sacrificial Lamb!"
JOHN 1:36 TPT

John the Baptist understood the importance of directing people to Christ rather than to himself. While John's actions may have seemed unconventional, he knew his role in preparing the way for the Savior. Your purpose is akin to John's: consistently point others to Christ. When your loved ones become Jesus' disciples, you release them and encourage them to wholeheartedly pursue God.

Do you recognize God's presence in the lives of those around you?

YOUR WILL BE DONE

"Your kingdom come, your will be done.
On earth as it is in heaven."
MATTHEW 6:10 NIV

A kingdom used to be all about the king, and it could be good or bad depending on that king. Jesus is the best King. He triumphed over sin through his death and resurrection. As you align yourself with him, you take up the cause of his kingdom. Praying like Jesus causes thoughts and preferences to change. It means having a heart for the sick and the outcast, understanding sacrifice, and making Jesus your first allegiance.

Do your desires align with those of God's kingdom?

Restoring Others

If someone is caught in a sin, you who live by the Spirit should restore that person gently. But watch yourselves, or you also may be tempted.
Galatians 6:1 niv

You may be tempted to shape people according to your own desires. If you enforce right choices, it only yields temporary compliance without fostering true faith or independent decision-making. Instead, gently mentor people, allowing natural consequences to unfold. Lovingly help them to understand the importance of their choices.

Do you seek God's guidance in cultivating gentleness while mentoring others?

DAILY BREAD

"Give us today our daily bread."
MATTHEW 6:11 NIV

God is not only concerned with spiritual needs; he is interested in everything and even made our food. Previous generations had an intimate relationship with their food. They raised their meat and grew their vegetables. They depended on the rain and the sun. While you easily buy a loaf of bread, previous generations grew the wheat and made each loaf from scratch. Recognize that God is the God of every bit of creation. And remember that even a slice of toast in the morning is a gift.

Do you appreciate the simple blessing of your daily food?

THIS CHILD

"She will give birth to a son, and you are to give him the name Jesus, because he will save his people from their sins."

MATTHEW 1:21 NIV

Joy to the world, the Lord has come! When Christ came as a little child, he not only brought joy to the people of the day, he also brought joy to the entire world. You celebrate because you know the significance of Christ being born as a human, entering into the world, and displaying what it meant to be fully alive. The restoration that Christ brings is why you can have joy on this day.

How can you express joy today as you celebrate Christ's birth?

BEAUTIFUL DIFFICULTY

"Forgive us our debts,
as we have also forgiven our debtors."
MATTHEW 6:12 NIV

Forgiveness sounds beautiful, but it is awkward to practice. Forgiveness is necessary in your life, both from you toward others and from others for you. However, the best picture of forgiveness—the most beautiful of difficulties—is the cross. On the cross, Jesus bore the weightiness of all your sin, and he offered the beautiful gift of divine forgiveness. When you understand that, your call to forgiveness becomes a little less difficult.

Do you remember Jesus forgave you, so you forgive those who hurt you?

A Bigger Story

An angel of the Lord appeared to him in a dream and said, "Joseph son of David, do not be afraid to take Mary home as your wife, because what is conceived in her is from the Holy Spirit."

MATTHEW 1:20 NIV

Joseph faced a challenging situation. His betrothed was pregnant, but the child wasn't his. Despite the risk to his reputation and livelihood, he still loved her and didn't want to shame her. He could have quietly ended the relationship, but an angel appeared and reassured him that a greater story was unfolding; he needn't be afraid.

Do you love and serve others in light of your relationship with God?

LEAD US NOT

> "Lead us not into temptation,
> but deliver us from the evil one."
> MATTHEW 6:13 NIV

It's easy to focus on a temptation when you are struggling to overcome it, or it is a topic of discussion. The solution to overcoming temptation is to focus on something better than that which is tempting you. Scripture speaks about fixing your eyes on Jesus. Why? Because then your gaze is on something far better than the diversions of culture. Indeed, your gaze is on the one your heart truly craves.

Are you able to take your eyes away from temptations and focus on Jesus?

Slave No Longer

You are no longer a slave but a son,
and if a son, then God has made you an heir.
GALATIANS 4:7 CSB

Going from slave to son is a monumental shift. You have been granted a privileged position. It's not a matter of obligation. You walk alongside God as he affectionately calls you his son. The relationship you have with God through Christ is an incredible opportunity. You can sit face-to-face having conversations and a relationship that only a Father can give to a child.

When you are discouraged, do you remember that you belong to God?

BE ONE

"That all of them may be one, Father,
just as you are in me and I am in you."
JOHN 17:21 NIV

Teams rise or fall based on how relationally unified they are. Bad
relationships fracture teams and lead to failure. Although the 2004 U.S.
Olympic basketball team had the best players in the world, they fell short
of the gold medal because each member wanted to be the star. When voices
harmonize, beautiful music results. Jesus prays that his disciples will be one
because he wants harmony, not fracture.

Are you in harmony with God's will in your relationships?

GOD IS FAITHFUL

God is faithful; you were called by him into fellowship
with his Son, Jesus Christ our Lord.

1 CORINTHIANS 1:9 CSB

Some guarantees hold more value than others. Lifetime guarantees may only last a few years, and some aren't worth the paper they were written on. The value of a guarantee lies in the integrity of the person behind it. The guarantee presented here surpasses the value of any material possession. It assures you of freedom from sin and guilt because it comes directly from God.

Are you grateful to God for his faithfulness in keeping his promises?

PROOF

"May they also be in us so that the world
may believe that you have sent me."

JOHN 17:21 NIV

After hearing the advertisements and making the purchase, it really only matters if the product performs as promised. If the product fails, the advertising and purchase were a failure. Jesus prays for unity amongst believers because if the church is unified, the world will believe. The proof of the church is in the unity of its members. The skeptical world needs to see God's love.

Do you radiate God's love so the world will know him?

FILLED TO OVERFLOWING

May the God of hope fill you with all joy and peace as you believe so that
you may overflow with hope by the power of the Holy Spirit.

ROMANS 15:13 CSB

Your hope, joy, and peace are not superficial; they come from God to fill you
completely. Your hope is meant to overflow to those around you as you are
driven by the Holy Spirit. You can bring hope to others as God gives you
opportunities to share the gospel.

Do you earnestly seek the abundant presence of hope?

OUR HELPER

"I have given them the glory that you gave me,
that they may be one as we are one."
JOHN 17:22 NIV

Have you been asked to do something without the resources to accomplish it? Jesus has thankfully not left you without his help! He said that Christian unity is attainable only because he has placed his presence in each believer. Unity happens as you yield to the Holy Spirit. You have to lay down your agenda. If you want the unity that Christ has prayed for, you have to claim, "Not my will, but yours."

Do you seek the presence of God through his Spirit?

GOOD WORDS

"A good man brings good things out of the good stored up in his heart, and an evil man brings evil things out of the evil stored up in his heart. For the mouth speaks what the heart is full of."

LUKE 6:45 NIV

To speak good words, your heart must be filled with good and absent of evil. Confess your sins to God, allowing your heart to be filled by him. Make this a daily practice. Ask God to reveal any traces of evil, confess them, and seek his goodness. Keep your heart filled with Christ so you speak goodness to loved ones.

Do you speak words of goodness to your loved ones?

ONE BODY

In Christ we, though many, form one body,
and each member belongs to all the others.
ROMANS 12:5 NIV

A bicycle has many parts: handlebars for turning, pedals for moving, and brakes for stopping. If you were missing one the bike wouldn't work. Consider the people around you. Some love administration; others love people. Pioneers challenge your faith. Creatives inspire awe. Straight shooters tell you what you need to hear. If you took away any one type from your family, church, or workplace, the difference would be noticeable.

Do you value the diversity of the people God placed in your life?

FORGIVENESS

"Don't be grieved or angry with yourselves for selling me here,
because God sent me ahead of you to preserve life."
GENESIS 45:5 CSB

Imagine being sold as a slave, falsely accused, and imprisoned. Joseph
experienced horrific challenges because his brothers hated him. Yet he
forgave them and urged them to also forgive themselves. Despite countless
opportunities to dwell on the wrongdoings, Joseph didn't succumb to
bitterness. God's grace granted him a fresh perspective.

Do you recognize the importance of forgiveness?

LEGACY

"My prayer is not for them alone.
I pray also for those who will believe in me through their message."
JOHN 17:20 NIV

What do you think of when you hear the word *legacy*? Jesus prayed a legacy prayer as the time of the cross got closer. He didn't pray for himself though he was in the middle of crisis. He didn't pray for his followers though they would soon face crisis. Jesus, in one of his last moments on earth, thought about you. Leaving a legacy brings you closer to understanding the mind of Christ.

Do you have a God-sized vision of future generations?

WHAT IS RIGHT

When his master heard the story his wife told him…
he was furious and had him thrown into prison.
GENESIS 39:19-20 CSB

The world will tell you to do the right thing because it promises a good outcome. God, however, tells you to do the right thing simply because it's right. You likely want others to know that your commitment is to doing right regardless of the cost. Whether others see it or not, doing the right thing will always be the right thing.

Is your desire to do what is right motivated by a desire to please God?

PILGRIMAGE

Blessed are those whose strength is in you,
whose hearts are set on pilgrimage.
PSALM 84:5 NIV

A good way to tell what you have set your heart on is to notice what you think about often or where you spend your money and time. The psalmist said that the blessed have set their hearts *pilgrimage*, meaning they pursue something with real meaning. The man who sets his heart on pilgrimage knows his weaknesses and moral deficiencies and is seeking to grow in those areas.

Do you have a purposeful pilgrimage as your life's goal?

BOLD FAITH

"Perhaps the LORD will be with me
and I will drive them out as the LORD promised."
JOSHUA 14:12 CSB

At eighty-five years old, Caleb had already experienced years of wilderness wandering and fighting to reach the Promised Land. Despite the battles, he didn't retreat; he clung to God's promise. God doesn't always choose the youngest, fastest, or most equipped to fulfill his will. He looks for those who recall his promises and declare, "I will conquer these challenges because God has guaranteed my victory."

How assured are you of God's promises?

HEARTBROKEN

"When I heard these things, I sat down and wept."
NEHEMIAH 1:4 NIV

Experiencing something deeply upsetting can be difficult, but it can also propel you toward action. Men who act because of a grave need create a positive impact from a negative situation. When Nehemiah heard that his hometown was destroyed, he returned and started the restoration work. He surveyed the problem and understood the need. He gathered people and persevered through challenges. Be driven to action by something that breaks your heart.

What breaks your heart?

PASS THE FAITH

"This may be a sign among you. When your children ask in time to come, 'What do those stones mean to you?' then you shall tell them that the waters of the Jordan were cut off before the ark of the covenant of the LORD."

JOSHUA 4:6-7 ESV

God understands how easily you can forget the amazing things he has done for you, such as providing financially or physically. Just as God instructed the Israelites to build memorials, you too can establish modern memorials to pass down the narratives of your faith.

Do you rely on God's assistance to recall his mighty deeds?

OPPOSITION

*"What they are building—even a fox climbing up on it
would break down their wall of stones!"*
NEHEMIAH 4:3 NIV

How do you handle opposition? Are you pushed around, or do you lash back? Perseverance is difficult. When you make a positive impact, you will encounter opposition. It comes through self-doubt and distractions, and from critics and skeptics. Perseverance, though, begins with prayer. When you pray, God reminds you of the urgency of your tasks, so you find the strength to keep going.

Are you persevering by praying to God who strengthens you?

RITES OF PASSAGE

"The LORD bless you and keep you;
the LORD make his face shine on you
and be gracious to you;
the LORD turn his face toward you
and give you peace."

NUMBERS 6:24-26 NIV

God instructed Moses to teach Aaron these words of blessing for the people of Israel. Since then, they have been repeated as a heartfelt blessing. God hears and answers this prayer. Pray it over people in your life.

Do you pray for God's abundant mercy to surround your loved ones?

CHRIST IN ME

I have been crucified with Christ and I no longer live,
but Christ lives in me.
GALATIANS 2:20 NIV

"Who am I?" is a question that has a variety of answers. You can define yourself by what you did or didn't do, but deriving identity from achievements can cause a crisis as you realize your limitations and weaknesses. The very core of you is connected to Jesus Christ. He provides your identity. Because of that, you are accepted despite any achievements or lack thereof.

Are you clear about what defines you?

SAVED BY MERCY

He saved us, not because of the righteous things we had done, but because of his mercy. He washed away our sins, giving us a new birth and new life through the Holy Spirit.

TITUS 3:5 NLT

Salvation is not earned through any effort on your part but solely by God's mercy. As you embrace this truth, your faith deepens. Your righteous actions flow from your salvation, not as any means to obtain it. You do what is right in response to God's mercy.

How do you seek a deeper understanding of God's mercy?

STATUS SYMBOL

There is neither Jew nor Gentile, neither slave nor free,
nor is there male and female, for you are all one in Christ Jesus.
GALATIANS 3:28 NIV

Paul dismantled status symbols. A slave was as important as a free person. A Jew was the same as a Gentile. A woman was on the same level as a man. No one was above another. You are in the same desperate situation; in Christ you are given more than you can imagine. The ultimate status symbol is the cross.

Do you rely on God for your status?

EQUIPPING

Fight the good fight of the faith. Take hold of eternal life to which you were called and about which you have made a good confession in the presence of many witnesses.

1 TIMOTHY 6:12 CSB

Every day you face temptations to compromise your integrity. This struggle is not unique to you. The fight of faith is often an internal one. You may question your convictions, but it's important to hold on to your salvation. Each day you may find yourself battling to stand firm in your faith but take heart: it's a battle worth fighting.

Do you courageously stand for what is righteous and true?

FREEDOM

It is for freedom that Christ has set us free. Stand firm, then,
and do not let yourselves be burdened again by a yoke of slavery.
GALATIANS 5:1 NIV

People love stories about being freed from captivity. Paul challenged the
Galatians because their faith was about the rules, but true faith means
freedom from religious regulations. You may love the idea of being freed from
rule-based religion, or self-criticism, or the approval of others, but there is
more to freedom than escaping something. True freedom is achieved through
Christ's work on the cross and for the purpose of loving God and the world.

Are you alert to what your freedom in God means?

INTERCESSION

First of all, then, I urge that petitions, prayers, intercessions,
and thanksgivings be made for everyone.
1 TIMOTHY 2:1 CSB

You're likely used to praying for the people close to you, but in Paul's letter
to Timothy he says to include everyone. Prayer is far-reaching and powerful
for salvation and knowledge of the truth. You know people around you who
need the love of the Savior, but countless others you've never met also need
it. Through prayer, you join in God's work. Intercede for people worldwide,
beyond your circle. Ask God to intervene and reveal himself to them.

Can you pray for God's revelation to those who are desperately in need of him?

INVITATION

After this I saw a vast crowd, too great to count, from every nation and tribe and people and language, standing in front of the throne and before the Lamb.

REVELATION 7:9 NIV

When John, the author of Revelation, got a glimpse into heaven, people from all places, groups, and backgrounds were standing next to each other. Jesus' invitation to his eternal celebration isn't limited; everyone is invited. Although invitations now have understandable limits, are you living fully with the knowledge that all have been invited to the heavenly banquet?

Have you accepted the invitation to the eternal celebration with God?

SALVATION THROUGH CHRIST

Here is a trustworthy saying that deserves full acceptance:
Christ Jesus came into the world to save sinners—of whom I am the worst.
1 TIMOTHY 1:15 NIV

Jesus came to save sinners. Paul once approved the persecution of believers, but he acknowledged the grace he had received. You also no longer live condemned because your sins were forgiven on the cross. Embrace the freedom that comes from knowing that Christ Jesus came to save sinners like you.

How does the assurance of complete forgiveness impact your life?

EVANGELISM

Pray for us, too, that God will give us many opportunities to speak about his mysterious plan concerning Christ. That is why I am here in chains.
COLOSSIANS 4:3 NLT

Evangelism can cause anxiety especially if you don't know what to say. Paul asked the church in Colossae to pray for open doors, not to barge through them. Everyone who has heard the good news is called to pass it on. It requires patient prayer. It involves long-term relationships which allow God to open the door of an unbeliever's heart. It means saying, "How can I pray for you?"

Do you have good, long-term relationships with unbelievers?

ENCOURAGEMENT MATTERS

Encourage one another and build each other up as you are already doing.
1 THESSALONIANS 5:11 CSB

Encouraging words have the power to inspire and refuel you. Today's Scripture encourages you to be a source of encouragement to others. While criticism may seem like a motivator, an encouraging word has far-reaching effects. Expressing your appreciation and love to those close to you can be genuinely uplifting.

Are you actively seeking opportunities to encourage those around you?

QUALIFYING

"Go. I am sending you to Pharaoh."
But Moses said to God, "Who am I?"
EXODUS 3:10-11

Fear plagued Moses when God called him to lead the Israelites to freedom. And his concern wasn't unfounded because he wasn't really qualified. He stuttered, skipped town after killing someone, and didn't truly fit leadership. Remember God is with you, and it is he who qualifies you. As you seek him, he will guide you.

Do you trust God to qualify you despite your own doubts?

TIME WITH GOD

The news about him spread even more, and large crowds would come together to hear him and to be healed of their sicknesses. Yet he often withdrew to deserted places and prayed.

LUKE 5:15-16 CSB

Your primary focus should be cultivating a strong relationship with God. This may mean waking up early or staying up late to engage in meaningful conversations with the Father. Spending time communing with your heavenly Father is the most valuable and impactful action you can do for the kingdom and yourself.

When is it best for you to spend time alone with God?

CHALLENGE AND GROWTH

These have come so that the proven genuineness of your faith—of greater worth than gold, which perishes even though refined by fire—may result in praise, glory and honor when Jesus Christ is revealed.

1 PETER 1:7 NIV

Lifting weights will make you sore. Working on a strained relationship will create tough conversations. Buying a house requires saving for a down payment. You would probably like maturity to come easily, but challenges and growth are inseparable. You become pure and strong when you face opposition regarding your faith. What you have in Christ is worth more than gold.

Do you have eyes to see how God is maturing you?

LONGING FOR GOD

As a deer pants for flowing streams,
so pants my soul for you, O God.
PSALM 42:1 ESV

When you're thirsty, it's your body's way of signaling the need for hydration. You've learned to recognize the signs: dry mouth, itchy throat, that craving for liquid. To quench your physical thirst, you drink. But can you recognize the signs when your soul is thirsty? It may manifest as a short temper, unkind words, or feeling distant from God. Like a deer runs to a river to drink, run toward God and let his living waters restore your soul.

In what ways can you become more aware of the signs of a thirsty soul?

DESIRING GOD

Though you have not seen him, you love him;
and even though you do not see him now,
you believe in him and are filled with an inexpressible and glorious joy.
1 PETER 1:8 NIV

The recipients of Peter's letter never met Jesus face-to-face, but when they heard about him something changed them. They loved Jesus and were joyful as they anticipated eternity with him. They experienced a growing desire for Jesus because they held him and his Word before themselves, and this gave them great joy.

How are you growing in your desire to be near God?

SHELTER AND STRENGTH

God is our refuge and strength,
a helper who is always found
in times of trouble.
PSALM 46:1-3 CSB

In the middle of a world that seems to be falling apart with heartbreaking events, calamitous weather, and personal struggles, remember God is your refuge. He is with you now, and every detail is working toward his plan. He is your shelter when storms rage. Take comfort in knowing that he provides support and solace in the middle of everyday and extraordinary chaos.

Are you finding refuge and strength in God?

GET AWAY

Very early in the morning, while it was still dark, Jesus got up,
left the house and went off to a solitary place, where he prayed.
MARK 1:35 NIV

Jesus' first priority was not the crowd. He loved them, but his primary
concern was his Father. He knew that that relationship was where his strength
originated. Any healing or hope in the crowds rested on his interaction with
the Spirit and the Father. Popularity with men didn't define him. He heard his
Father's voice and welcomed the Spirit's presence as the most important thing.

How can you hear the voice of your Father over the opinions of everyone else?

DEVOTION TO JESUS

When they observed the boldness of Peter and John and realized that they were uneducated and untrained men, they were amazed and recognized that they had been with Jesus.

ACTS 4:13 CSB

Peter and John amazed the Jewish leaders with their words despite being considered ordinary and uneducated. They silenced their accusers and fearlessly proclaimed the truth of the gospel. The rulers were astonished by the undeniable truth spoken by these men. They couldn't argue or refute it. You can have the same devotion by spending time in the presence of Christ.

How can you cultivate boldness in proclaiming God's truth?

THE CALL TO WORK

The Lord God took the man and put him in the Garden of Eden
to work it and take care of it.
GENESIS 2:15 NIV

Early in Genesis, God gave his stamp of approval for work. This may be contrary
to what you've thought regarding the garden of Eden. Wouldn't paradise involve
sunglasses and tropical drinks? Maybe, but it also requires work. Because you
are made in the image of God and God worked as he created the world, you, too,
were created to work. God placed you in your workplace just as he placed Adam
in the garden. What would it look like to honor him there?

How can you respond to God's invitation to love both him and people?

CALLED TO SHARE

Those who were scattered went on their way preaching the word.
ACTS 8:4 CSB

The first-century believers who fled both Roman and Jewish persecution weren't church leaders or recognized preachers. They were Spirit-filled followers of Christ compelled, despite the threat of torture and death, to share the love of Jesus with others. You can begin by sharing it with your family. The more you know Jesus, the more equipped you are to proclaim his good news!

In what ways can you effectively share the good news of God's love?

HIDING

The man and his wife heard the sound of the LORD God as he was walking in the garden in the cool of the day, and they hid from the LORD God among the trees of the garden.

GENESIS 3:8 NIV

When you see someone you have unresolved conflict with, do you hide? When your boss asks how a big project is progressing, do you distract? The Bible says the tendency to hide is sourced in shame; you don't want others to see your real challenges. The way to heal shame is to stop hiding. That will deal your sin a decisive blow.

Do you honestly face the tendency to hide sin with a close relationship to God?

FORGIVENESS

Be kind and loving to each other,
and forgive each other just as God forgave you in Christ.
EPHESIANS 4:32 NCV

You might believe that forgiveness should only be given when it's requested. You may be challenged to show kindness and love to people who aren't nice. This way of living brings freedom from bitterness and unforgiveness. Remember, Christ forgave your sins on the cross long before you had the opportunity to seek it.

What does it look like for you to extend forgiveness to others?

JESUS HEALS

A man with leprosy came to him and begged him on his knees,
"If you are willing, you can make me clean."
MARK 1:40 NIV

In the Bible, people with leprosy couldn't enter the temple or live at home because of the risk of infection. Rabbis wouldn't get closer than six feet. Mark's leper walked right up to Jesus. Jesus was indignant, but it was not directed at the leper; it was at his condition. With the crowd watching, Jesus touched him. He could have healed from a distance or dismissed him for not following protocol. Instead, Jesus said, "I am willing."

Do you seek to be close to Jesus and his healing touch?

SUFFICIENCY OF GOD

"I am the Alpha and the Omega," says the Lord God,
"the one who is, who was, and who is to come, the Almighty."
REVELATION 1:8 CSB

Do you wonder or worry about the future? God has all the answers to your questions. In the middle of your concerns, he assures you he is coming back. He has a complete understanding of time and power, and he holds the answers you seek. As you gaze into the unknown future, understand that God firmly holds it in his hands as the all-powerful God.

Can you find true rest and comfort in God's assurance?

NEEDING JESUS

"It is not the healthy who need a doctor, but the sick.
I have not come to call the righteous, but sinners."
MARK 2:17 NIV

Healthy people don't require a doctor. Believers who think they're doing well and don't need the Great Physician are tragic. Your relationship with God isn't based on your goodness but on your confession of need for Jesus. Followers of Jesus are called to reach the spiritually sick. Your goal is to seek those in need rather than to protect yourself. Everyone needs the Great Physician.

How can you love the spiritually sick just as Jesus did?

INTEGRITY

"If we are thrown into the blazing furnace, the God whom we serve is able to save us. He will rescue us from your power, Your Majesty. But even if he doesn't, we want to make it clear to you, Your Majesty, that we will never serve your gods or worship the gold statue you have set up."

DANIEL 3:17-18 NLT

Unwavering in their allegiance to God, these three men prioritized their integrity, valuing it more than their own lives. Their assurance came by walking with God and placing their hopes solely in him. In the face of moral decay, you can demonstrate such unwavering resolve. Stand firm.

How can you cultivate a life of integrity?

IN FAITH

"But what about you?" he asked. "Who do you say I am?"
Peter answered, "You are the Messiah."
MARK 8:29 NIV

Some people find it easy to take faith-filled steps while others are paralyzed by the pressure. Peter felt the pressure when Jesus asked the disciples, "Who do you say I am?" He wanted them to boldly share who they believed him to be. They had seen Jesus heal, teach, calm, and perform other miracles. It was courageous and faithful Peter who said that Jesus is the Messiah. The proverb says, "Fortune favors the bold." What is Jesus inviting you to risk today?

Is God calling you to step out in faith?

PIERCING THE HEART

The word of God is living and active, sharper than any two-edged sword,
piercing to the division of soul and of spirit, of joints and of marrow,
and discerning the thoughts and intentions of the heart.
HEBREWS 4:12 ESV

Sharing your faith with others can be challenging. It's common to feel
intimidated or unprepared, but you possess a powerful tool—the Word of
God. It has the ability to penetrate deeply. The more you familiarize yourself
with it, the easier it becomes to impart its wisdom. A simple verse can
illuminate motives and allow you to engage in conversations about faith.

What can you do to effectively share the wisdom of the Word with others?

COMMITTED

"Come," he replied,
"and you will see."
JOHN 1:39 NIV

You didn't know everything about your best friend when you met, nor do you now. There are dynamics that are exposed over time. As you learn about each other, characteristics eventually become predictable. This same pattern exists with God. When Jesus invited his followers to journey with him, he said, "Come, and you will see." As you take steps following Jesus, you see his predictable kindness and his reliable provision.

Are your eyes open to seeing God today, wherever he is leading?

THE THRONE ROOM

Let us approach the throne of grace with boldness,
so that we may receive mercy and find grace to help us in time of need.
HEBREWS 4:16 CSB

If you have ever wanted a VIP status or a key to the executive suite, you'll understand the honor of being a child of God. Through Jesus, you receive access to God's throne room. Imagine walking in as if you own the place, approaching the throne of grace without fear. You don't need to worry about credentials. Christ has everything you need.

Can you find boldness to approach the throne room of God?

HUMILITY

"After me comes the one more powerful than I."
MARK 1:7 NIV

John the Baptist's message was remarkable because everyone in both city and countryside was hanging on his every word. He set an example for the followers of Jesus. It's easy to get sucked into a self-absorbed approach because that is promoted in this culture. But John the Baptist wasn't focused on the adoring crowds or his own eloquence. Humility happens when your focus is on the one more powerful than you.

Are you capable of ridding yourself of self-focus?

MINDFUL OF WORDS

Do not be hasty to speak, and do not be impulsive to make a speech before God. God is in heaven and you are on earth, so let your words be few.

ECCLESIASTES 5:2 CSB

Be mindful of your words and don't speak before you think. Sometimes you realize the impact of your words as soon as you have spoken them, sometimes it's much later. Be careful that you don't give advice to others while neglecting your own guidance. Understand that God fully knows you and fully loves you. Be sincere in your worship, for God sees you and accepts you.

Do you practice restraining your words?

OPEN UP

How long, LORD, must I call for help,
but you do not listen?
HABAKKUK 1:2 NIV

Habakkuk called for God but didn't hear anything back. He shared his broken heart and didn't hold back. Throughout his exchange with God, he gradually found himself content, even without all his hopes fulfilled. It's when you dare to ask God the tough questions about pain and confusion that he can begin to heal and transform you.

Are you hiding pain or confusion that you should be sharing with God?

DIFFICULT LOVE

"My command is this: Love each other as I have loved you."
JOHN 15:12 NIV

It's easy to love people who already love you; it's harder to love those who act like jerks. Jesus' disciples were comprised of a possibly unethical tax collector, smelly fishermen, a doctor, and more. Yet Jesus loved them just as he loves you. Love your cheating coworker who received the promotion you deserved; love your neighbor with the annoying dog. Love them because Christ loves you, and they need Christ.

Have you asked Jesus for help to love those who are difficult?

WORKERS

"The harvest is plentiful but the workers are few.
Ask the Lord of the harvest, therefore,
to send out workers into his harvest."
MATTHEW 9:37-38 NIV

Even with a need for workers, Jesus didn't mount a marketing campaign, craft an elevator pitch, or hire a consultant. Jesus invited his followers to acknowledge that prayer is the first and most important step in the face of the world's overwhelming needs. The priority is to ask the Lord of the harvest to provide for the needs.

Do you ask God to address the needs around the world and in your city?

FAITHFULLY COMMITTED

Jesus Christ is the same yesterday, today, and forever.
HEBREWS 13:8 NLT

Jesus never left a project unfinished. He never started something and walked away because he got bored or things became too difficult. Jesus and his mission are the same yesterday, today, and forever. You may feel like a has-been or a mere glimmer of your former self, but Jesus is still committed to his relationship with you. Jesus is going to fulfill his plan for your life because he is and will be devoted to you!

Are you aware that Jesus is still with you during your darkest days?

RESET MY SOUL

In the beginning God created the heavens and the earth.
GENESIS 1:1 NIV

Pain and problems are experienced differently when you understand who is in control. You have an important role to play, but the hero in your story is not you. Weighty issues can pull you away from God's presence and it becomes difficult to see past your problems. Remember that in the beginning God created the heavens and the earth. He is in control—not you or any other person.

Do you believe that God is the author of creation?

RELATIONSHIP RESTORATION

Restore to me the joy of your salvation
and grant me a willing spirit, to sustain me.
PSALM 51:12 NIV

The Psalmist understood the brokenness in his relationship with God. He knew that being separated from the Lord was the worst thing imaginable. Yet, he also knew that seeking forgiveness and appealing for mercy from a loving God was the only path to restoration.

Will you ask your Father to restore the joy of his salvation within you?

TRAINED EARS

"Go and lie down, and if he calls you, say,
'Speak, LORD, for your servant is listening.'"
1 SAMUEL 3:9 NIV

A musically trained ear hears more than the average person. A musician will hear texture and rhythm, and understand the fullness of the music. Eli recognized God's voice, but Samuel did not have a trained ear yet. Eli taught Samuel to listen for and respond to the voice of the Lord. It's important to listen for God's voice and to disciple others to do the same. You can trust God to teach you to develop ears that hear the fullness of his music.

Have you asked God to teach you to hear his voice?

GREED

Then he said to them, "Watch out! Be on your guard against all kinds of greed; life does not consist in an abundance of possessions."

LUKE 12:15 NIV

All earthly purchases lose their value, most within a short time. This season, give gifts of lasting worth. Share the true meaning of Christmas, spread the love of Christ, share the hope of the gospel, and create lasting memories with family and friends. Move beyond materialism and embrace the joy of meaningful giving.

How do you guard against greed in this season?

STRENGTH

The LORD is my shepherd;
I have all that I need.
PSALM 23:1 NLT

Propaganda attempts to convince you that something is missing from your life. It tries to get you to think that owning more will give you what you need. Having new things is not the problem. The heart of the matter is believing that your fulfillment comes from what you possess, not who you follow. Strength is found in the simplicity of your needs—the Lord alone. Anything else is extra.

Do you seek to desire God alone?

GIVING THANKS

Whatever you do or say, do it as a representative of the Lord Jesus,
giving thanks through him to God the Father.
COLOSSIANS 3:17 NLT

Your every word and thought should reflect the character of Jesus. Everything
you do and say should flow from a heart of gratitude. Consider keeping
a gratitude journal or expressing thankfulness daily to those around you.
Notice how it transforms you. Enjoy this role of representing the Lord.

How do your words reflect the heart and character of Jesus?

GUIDANCE

Your word is a lamp to my feet
and a light to my path.
PSALM 119:105 ESV

It's tempting to allow the question, "What's next?" to direct your path, and, "Now what?" to determine your pace. Those priorities allow opportunistic thinking to be your guide. It's a human tendency to want headlights; God's Word is a lamp which will only light the next few steps of your journey. Looking ahead too far may make your feet move too quickly or in the wrong direction, and you may forget who you're walking with.

Do you give God control over the direction and pace of your path?

FEAR NOT

"Fear not, for I am with you;
be not dismayed, for I am your God.
I will strengthen you, yes, I will help you,
I will uphold you with My righteous right hand."

Isaiah 41:10 NKJV

When you face fears of the future, of insignificance, or of failure, remind yourself that you are truly not alone. God has promised to be with you, and he will provide the strength you need to face any situation. You can take shelter in his presence.

Will you seek comfort, encouragement, and strength by resting in God's presence?

TRUST IN THE LORD

Trust in the LORD with all your heart,
and do not lean on your own understanding.
PROVERBS 3:5 ESV

You will be spiritually unsatisfied if you acknowledge the Lord in some ways, but then try to pull yourself through life by leaning on your own understanding. It will affect your level of anxiety and cause confusion and conflict. God's grace steps in when you take yourself out of the equation and place your trust in him, acknowledging the Lord in all your ways.

Do you try to exhale your own control and stand before God with open hands and an open heart?

SENT

Calling the Twelve to him, he began to send them out two by two
and gave them authority over impure spirits.
MARK 6:7 NIV

Serving Jesus is a big responsibility. Jesus only called those who were chosen by God, and they were a mixed bag of personalities and capabilities. Jesus prayed over his men and sent them out with his authority. You have the presence of the Holy Spirit in you to ensure that you are fully equipped and prepared for any conversation or battle you may encounter.

Have you prayed for the Lord to replace your doubts with confidence in him?

USE MY WORDS

The tongue can bring death or life;
those who love to talk will reap the consequences.
PROVERBS 18:21 NLT

Words can crush a spirit. When you are attentive to what you say, you can heal the hurting, restore the weary, and create community. Loose lips, however, can cause division and destruction. Words cannot be unsaid. You can try to clean up the mess, but you can't take back what was said. When you understand that your words have the power to bring life or death, you become responsible for them.

Are you quick to listen and slow to speak?

STORYTELLING

"Go home to your own people and tell them how much the Lord has done for you, and how he has had mercy on you."
MARK 5:19 NIV

Storytelling has always been the primary way faith has been transferred from one generation to the next. Unfortunately, it has become a bit of a lost art. Scripture reveals that it is God's plan for us to share his praiseworthy deeds with future generations. You don't need special qualifications; you simply need to rediscover and tell your own story.

Will you share stories of hope that tell how God has changed your life?

SURRENDER

You can make many plans,
but the LORD's purpose will prevail.
PROVERBS 19:21 NLT

Planning prepares you for an uncertain future, but sometimes you need to put your plans in perspective. How many times has life turned out as planned? The most difficult part of planning is surrendering them to God's purposes. It is good to make plans, but when you bind yourself to them you risk God's disappointment. When you pursue God with the freedom to have your plans fail, you are embracing the Lord's purposes.

Do you keep in mind when planning that God's plans will prevail?

JESUS, MESSIAH

"Why are you so afraid?
Do you still have no faith?"
MARK 4:40 NIV

The Israelites had a complicated relationship with water. They were delivered through the Red Sea but still feared the power of Noah's flood. Isaiah prophesied about the coming Messiah and his connection to water, assuring them that he would always be with them. When Jesus calmed the storm, he referenced these promises, declaring himself to be the Promised One.

Will you surrender your fears in God's redeeming presence?

BE MY LIGHT

Do not gloat over me, my enemies!
For though I fall, I will rise again.
Though I sit in darkness, the LORD will be my light.
MICAH 7:8 NLT

Your strength is not determined by your failures or your mistakes. Rather, it is found in your source of power. If you subscribe to self-reliance, the ceiling of your strength is within your own greatest efforts. But if you find your strength in the Lord, you will overcome failure and stand fearlessly when darkness descends.

Is the Lord your source of light?

WELCOME TO THE FAMILY

"Whoever does God's will is my brother and sister and mother."
- MARK 3:35 NIV

There are issues in every family. Imperfections are a part of everyday life for every single person. Jesus had complicated family dynamics too. His ministry thrived, but his family thought he was crazy. Jesus taught his followers that family is redefined in his kingdom.

Are you pursuing God's will by supporting and encouraging others in their pursuit of God's will?

NO LONGER ANXIOUS

"I tell you, do not be anxious about your life, what you will eat or what you
will drink, nor about your body, what you will put on."
MATTHEW 6:25 ESV

Many things in life can consume your attention. There are so many perceived
problems to worry about, but if you understand the real issues and whose
hand you hold on your journey, you will experience peace. Some problems
seem significant in your eyes, but God has already taken care of them. You
can get distracted by your desires, but Jesus reminds you that your heavenly
Father values you more than even the birds.

Do you hold to God's perspective in the face of life's problems?

NEW THINGS

As he walked along, he saw Levi son of Alphaeus sitting at the tax collector's booth. "Follow me," Jesus told him, and Levi got up and followed him.
MARK 2:14 NIV

Jesus calls you even when you feel unpopular and isolated just as he called Levi the tax collector. It's amazing how despised people can find acceptance in unexpected places. Levi was identified by his family and occupation, but Jesus called him and changed his narrative. This liberating news changes you too. You aren't defined by your past. Jesus calls you to a new story.

Are you ready to embrace Jesus' call to follow him?

LOVE

Love is patient, love is kind. It does not envy, it does not boast, it is not proud. It does not dishonor others, it is not self-seeking, it is not easily angered, it keeps no record of wrongs. Love does not delight in evil but rejoices with the truth. It always protects, always trusts, always hopes, always perseveres.

1 CORINTHIANS 13:4-7 NIV

No single person can be the perfect example of love other than Jesus Christ. Don't shame yourself into thinking that if you fail at love, you have somehow upset God. It's just another moment in understanding how much you need God.

Do you have peace with your imperfect grasp of love, while relying on the perfect love of Jesus?

THE AMAZING NEWS

"The time has come," he said. "The kingdom of God has come near.
Repent and believe the good news!"
MARK 1:15 NIV

God is just a comment away. Repentance is a beautiful gift. It's a Spirit-led moment of realizing your own limitations and knowing that God's amazing grace is right there when you turn around. The King and his kingdom are within reach. Your cry for help has been answered by your loving heavenly Father.

Have you humbly acknowledged your reliance on God's power?

COMPASSION

When he saw the crowds, he had compassion for them,
because they were harassed and helpless, like sheep without a shepherd.
MATTHEW 9:36 ESV

Compassion grows naturally when you understand someone's story.
Compassion was Jesus' natural reaction when he saw the harassed and
helpless people in the crowds. Their circumstances did not change in that
moment, but their story did. Jesus entered their struggles making their
problems his own. If you seek to extend grace to those in need, compassion
will become part of your life.

Are you compassionate to those around you?

ALL YOU NEED

The Lord be with your spirit.
Grace be with you all.
2 TIMOTHY 4:22 NIV

It's another crazy day—driving, working, juggling responsibilities. It's non-stop and challenging! It feels like a long-distance race. God is with you, providing abundant grace. You may run out of steam, but God's resources are limitless. Your strength to overcome sin is small, but his grace is mighty. Remember the constant presence of Jesus and accept his abundant grace in your life.

Are you willing to surrender your stress to God?

LIFE WITH CHRIST

"Simply join your life with mine. Learn my ways and you'll discover that I'm gentle, humble, easy to please. You will find refreshment and rest in me."
MATTHEW 11:29 TPT

This life can lead you to work hard, play hard, crash hard, and pray hard. Jesus calls you to a new way which gives you proper rest. When oxen are yoked together, the stronger moves, and the weaker is pulled along. When you are yoked with Jesus, you labor together, and you benefit from his strength.

Are you able to rest in Christ's presence and benefit from his ways?

BROTHERHOOD

The Lord stood at my side and gave me strength,
so that through me the message might be fully proclaimed.

2 TIMOTHY 4:17 NIV

In ancient warfare, the men standing with you were crucial to whether you lived or died. Your battle mates were considered brothers. As a believer, you need to surround yourself with godly men. The fight of faith is too big to face alone. Your fellow disciples will care for you as you care for them.

Who stands by your side to fight with you?

COURAGE

"Take courage! It is I. Don't be afraid."
"Lord, if it's you," Peter replied, "tell me to come to you on the water."
MATTHEW 14:27-29 NIV

When you are distracted by a need for comfort, you are choosing to stay in the boat where your fears dictate your direction. Courage is not the absence of fear but the presence of peace when fear is at hand. When your object of hope is greater than your object of fear, you can be courageous. You experience peace when you put Jesus on the proper pedestal.

Are you aware of God's peace in the middle of your storms?

EYES ON THE PRIZE

I have fought the good fight, I have finished the race, I have kept the faith.
Now there is in store for me the crown of righteousness, which the Lord, the
righteous Judge, will award to me on that day—and not only to me, but also
to all who have longed for his appearing.

2 TIMOTHY 4:7-8 NIV

You were made for the fight. You're created for the long run. You learn in
the Word how to strategize and when to press on. You're stronger than you
realize. Stay focused on the eternal prize; listen to your coach, King Jesus. The
crown of righteousness awaits. Keep fighting and keep running.

Where do your courage and strength come from?

CREATIVITY

"To one he gave five talents, to another two, to another one,
to each according to his ability."
MATTHEW 25:14-15 ESV

It used to take a servant twenty years to earn a talent. Each one in today's verse had the opportunity to exercise creativity in an effort to make the master proud. You also have received gifts to be used for God. He guides you but without specific instructions. He gives you opportunities to be creative in order to make him proud of his investment in you.

Are you creative with your talents so they are used for God's glory?

FINISH THE JOB

Exercise self-control in everything, endure hardship,
do the work of an evangelist, fulfill your ministry.
2 TIMOTHY 4:5 CSB

When Paul encouraged Timothy to keep the message alive, he meant it was time to put it into action. Just as Jesus demonstrated the good news, you are also called to do so. Seek ways to speak the truth which you proclaim. Show those around you that you're not just a person with a book, but a person with a Word.

Can you demonstrate God's kingdom to the world?

PREPARATION

"You are my Son, whom I love; with you I am well pleased."
At once the Spirit sent him out into the wilderness.
MARK 1:11-12 NIV

Sometimes circumstances make you question God's motives and even doubt his love. In those wilderness seasons, it's important to have a posture of receiving and growing. When Jesus was baptized, God affirmed him, but immediately the Spirit led him into the wilderness. You don't have to question God's love when you find yourself struggling; trust the process and let the wilderness season prepare you for the future.

Are you allowing God to shape you in your wilderness seasons?

DON'T FOLLOW

The time will come when people will not tolerate sound doctrine, but according to their own desires, will multiply teachers for themselves because they have an itch to hear what they want to hear. They will turn away from hearing the truth and will turn aside to myths.

2 TIMOTHY 4:3-4 CSB

The temptation to follow the crowd will become increasingly pervasive. Be encouraged to step onto the field and secure the victory. It is your moment to shine. Despite the pressure to conform to cultural influences, remember that you also were created for sound doctrine which keeps your true calling alive.

How can you use your special calling to shine for Jesus today?

COMMITMENT

When they could not get near him because of the crowd, they removed the roof above him, and when they had made an opening, they let down the bed on which the paralytic lay.

MARK 2:4 ESV

When roadblocks impede your path, commitment is tested. If your commitment is stronger than any obstacle, you will be creative in completing the task. If your commitment is frail and your dedication is faint, you will quit. A commitment to helping others to the feet of Christ is worth fighting for.

Is your commitment tenacious enough to fight for your friends in their pursuit of Christ?

THE MAIN THING

Preach the word of God. Be prepared, whether the time is favorable or not. Patiently correct, rebuke, and encourage your people with good teaching.

2 TIMOTHY 4:2 NLT

Every man's life tells a unique story. Each decision, interaction, and effort leaves an impact. Align your story with God's story; it makes your impact resonate with God's purposes. Be encouraged to prioritize God's plan, remain open to his leading, and edify others through his knowledge.

How can you integrate God's Word into your story today?

PRESENCE IN STORMS

A furious squall came up, and the waves broke over the boat,
so that it was nearly swamped.
MARK 4:37 NIV

You can hope for bright days, but stormy skies are part of the journey. When Jesus took his disciples out on the lake, the winds picked up. When the waters rose, and the waves began to sink the boat, he was there. Jesus is in the storm with you. When sickness, loss, or confusion threatens to capsize you, he is your comforter.

Do you find comfort in Jesus whenever the struggle is real?

THE WORD

All Scripture is inspired by God and is profitable for teaching, for rebuking,
for correcting, for training in righteousness.

2 TIMOTHY 3:16 CSB

It's normal to feel unprepared for life's challenges. Amid the chaos and
uncertainties, remember to stand on these two foundations: God's Word and
the gift of salvation. Embrace the guidance and strength found in Scripture.
Hold onto the gift of salvation, knowing your life is secure in Christ.

Do you allow the Word of God to guide and equip you?

JUST BELIEVE

While Jesus was still speaking, some people came from the house of Jairus, the synagogue leader. "Your daughter is dead," they said. "Why bother the teacher anymore?"

MARK 5:35 NIV

When life doesn't go as planned, fear of the unknown can cause you to switch plans. Your doubts are reinforced by negativity. You can unknowingly give power to the critics who extinguish your hope. Jesus desires to pull you out of your hopelessness and beyond your fear. He wants you to put your faith in him. His words may not be louder than those of the critics, but they are more powerful.

Do you listen for God's voice when the critics are attacking?

KEEP GOING

Continue in what you have learned and have firmly believed,
knowing from whom you learned it.
2 TIMOTHY 3:14 ESV

Your investment in relationships, your dedication to your career, and your commitment to prayer and seeking God's presence are commendable. Take heart and be encouraged today. You're making a significant impact. You know your identity and purpose. Take a deep breath, focus on your energies, and reenter the battle. Embrace it today.

What motivates you to continue in your journey?

LIKE A CHILD

"Truly I tell you, anyone who will not receive the kingdom of God like a little child will never enter it."
MARK 10:15 NIV

Receiving the gift of the kingdom requires humility and forgiveness. Becoming "like a little child" is all that is needed for you to be grafted into the kingdom. Self-reliance can lead you to think that you are all you need, but a commitment to humility and forgiveness allows you receive eternal life in the kingdom with the King.

Are you taking steps to remain humble as a child of God?

BE FOCUSED

People will be lovers of self, lovers of money, boastful, proud, demeaning,
disobedient to parents, ungrateful, unholy.

2 TIMOTHY 3:2 CSB

While money is necessary for acquiring your basic needs, the Bible warns
that the love of money leads to various sins. Money itself isn't inherently
wrong, but problems arise when it becomes your focus instead of your tool
for provision. As you love God and follow his tenets, it will be to find the
right position for money in your life.

How can you ensure your heart isn't entangled with a love for money?

SERVANT LEADERSHIP

"Even the Son of Man did not come to be served, but to serve,
and to give his life as a ransom for many."
MARK 10:45 NIV

Culture might call you to climb the ladder of success, or to prize promotions and titles. You might find yourself using people for selfish benefits. Jesus presents a different pathway to power. He seeks your service and sacrifice because he is a sacrificial servant. When you take the path to Christ, you seek to put others ahead of yourself and build a culture that reflects the kingdom.

Do you have the eyes to see yourself honestly and serve as Christ served?

GET READY

You should know this, Timothy, that in the last days
there will be very difficult times.
2 TIMOTHY 3:1 NLT

Following Jesus means navigating complex relationships and unpredictable situations without guaranteed comfort or earthly safety. Your calling is an adventure that is filled with challenges and complications. It is your responsibility to navigate these experiences and to equip others to do the same.

Do you have courage to be a living example of trust in God?

AMAZING GRACE

"He arose and came to his father. But while he was still a long way off,
his father saw him and felt compassion,
and ran and embraced him and kissed him."
LUKE 15:20 ESV

When you sin, you may think you need to earn your way back. In the parable of the prodigal son, the father welcomed his son home with a celebration even though the son was prepared to work as a servant. The heavenly Father does the same for you. And once you receive his grace, you understand how to extend it to others.

Is it easy or difficult for you to understand God's amazing grace?

GET YOUR HANDS DIRTY

Hardworking farmers should be the first
to enjoy the fruit of their labor.
2 TIMOTHY 2:6 NLT

Paul compared a life of faith to that of a soldier, athlete, and farmer. A soldier seeks glory, an athlete pursues gold and fame, while a farmer toils in the mud but also knows the reward of the harvest. Embrace the hard work; you are close to the reward. Don't shy away from the challenges of manhood. Roll up your sleeves and dive in!

Are you praying for God to grant you a farmer's heart?

SACRIFICE

"There is no one who has left house or wife or brothers or parents or children, for the sake of the kingdom of God, who will not receive many times more in this time, and in the age to come eternal life."

LUKE 18:29-30 ESV

Sacrifice is not a light load. It entails loss which evokes pain. It also ushers in new life. Jesus doesn't call you to sacrifice for the sake of loss, but for the sake of the kingdom's gain. When you prioritize Christ, you'll see beyond the sacrifice. God promises that the benefits outweigh the loss not only now but also in the age to come.

Do you surrender all that you are and all that you have to Jesus?

BE UNDIVIDED

Athletes cannot win the prize
unless they follow the rules.
2 TIMOTHY 2:5 NLT

Throughout history, athletes have resorted to bribery, match fixing, and other dishonest tactics to gain an advantage. To be a true athlete, you must embody integrity and remain consistent on and off the field in a culture that promotes shortcuts. In other words, be the same person in your daily life as you are on the track.

Are you asking God to assist you in becoming a person of integrity?

ROUTINES

"Everyone who drinks of this water will be thirsty again, but whoever drinks of the water that I will give him will never be thirsty again. The water that I will give him will become in him a spring of water welling up to eternal life."
JOHN 4:13-14 ESV

Daily routines can condition you for comfort, but you can't settle and expect to change for Christ. Your heart will long for more, so don't settle for less. If you allow Jesus to disrupt your daily rhythm, you can develop eyes to see what Christ offers—a life that satisfies beyond your temporary desires.

Is your daily routine mindless or mindful of Jesus' plan for you?

BE LOYAL

No one serving as a soldier gets entangled in civilian affairs,
but rather tries to please his commanding officer.
2 TIMOTHY 2:4 NIV

You have already pledged your allegiance to King Jesus. The challenge from
Paul to Timothy was not about joining an army, but about remaining loyal. In
a world where loyalties shift constantly, remember that there is nothing better
than what you have in Christ. Death is defeated, sin is under your feet, and
glory awaits you. Don't be swayed by distractions. Humbly submit, receive
your orders, and walk in obedience.

Are you humbling yourself before the leadership of King Jesus?

CONSTANT PRESENCE

"I know that Messiah (called Christ) is coming.
When he comes, he will explain everything to us."
JOHN 4:25 NIV

It is possible to cling to God's promises in the middle of confusion. When you're blinded by expectations, Jesus is standing nearby even if you fail to recognize him. The woman above didn't know the details, but she knew the Messiah was coming to explain everything. When she declared her faith, Jesus revealed his identity. Life has doubts, but faith in the Messiah reveals his constant presence with you.

Do you put your faith in God when confusion and doubt overwhelm you?

BE BRAVE

God gave us a spirit not of fear
but of power and love and self-control.
2 TIMOTHY 1:7 ESV

Fear can grip and paralyze at any moment. The uncertainty of the future, mounting responsibilities, and the fear of rejection can be overwhelming. Invite the Spirit to be involved. Acknowledge fear without letting it paralyze you. Recognize that God dwells within you and empowers you with tools greater than fear: power, love, and self-control.

Do you believe that God is greater than everything you fear?

SMALL STUFF

What are mere mortals that you should think about them,
human beings that you should care for them?
PSALM 8:4 NLT

If you have ever watched a scientific program about the universe, you likely felt overwhelmed by how colossal and complex the universe and surrounding galaxies were! Earth is nothing in comparison to the vastness of the rest of the cosmos. Why would God care about you? He created you to live in relationship with him. Let his love overwhelm you today.

Do you feel significant to God?

PASSIONATE

I remind you to rekindle the gift of God that is in you
through the laying on of my hands.
2 TIMOTHY 1:6 CSB

The metaphor of a fire served well as a reminder to stoke the embers of faith.
Just as Timothy was called to reflect on his passion for his faith, it's now
your turn. Recall the times when your love for Jesus burned brightly and the
gospel consumed your heart. Take a moment to remember that passionate
faith. Seek God's help to rekindle that fire within you.

Have you asked God to reignite the fire within you?

PARTICIPATING

When Jesus looked up and saw a great crowd coming toward him, he said to Philip, "Where shall we buy bread for these people to eat?" He asked this only to test him, for he already had in mind what he was going to do.
JOHN 6:5-6 NIV

Good leaders anticipate and prepare for problems before they happen. Great leaders invite others into the solutions because there is value in others' participation. Servant leaders ask others for input. Jesus was certainly capable of performing the miracle by himself, but he chose to involve his disciples. Find the value in inviting others to be part of the solution.

How can you actively recruit others to be part of the answer?

BE REAL

I remember your genuine faith, for you share the faith that first filled your
grandmother Lois and your mother, Eunice. And I know that same faith
continues strong in you.
2 TIMOTHY 1:5 NLT

Are you genuine? Would people say you are authentic and true without any
hypocrisy? Align your words with your actions and live with unwavering
sincerity. When you authentically live your faith, it inspires hope and
admiration, and it exemplifies a clear path to follow. Continue to demonstrate
the genuine faith you want to see in your family and friends.

Do you desire to become a person of integrity?

EMBRACING ABUNDANCE

"A thief has only one thing in mind—he wants to steal, slaughter, and
destroy. But I have come to give you everything in abundance, more than
you expect—life in its fullness until you overflow!"
JOHN 10:10 TPT

Sometimes you struggle to get by, and daily existence lulls you into a trance.
Deep within, you know that you were created for more than the daily grind.
Your soul hungers for more, but you try to micromanage the circumstances.
Following Christ is the way out of that routine. You bring life to those around
you if you receive the life that Jesus offers.

Are you in survival mode or are you living abundantly?

CALLING

This letter is from Paul, chosen by the will of God to be an apostle of Christ Jesus. I have been sent out to tell others about the life he has promised through faith in Christ Jesus.

2 TIMOTHY 1:1 NLT

Do you struggle to stay focused amid the constant noise? Are you caught up in crises and endless activities? By keeping your eyes on the larger vision, the smaller details will fall into place. Reflect on this Scripture especially in challenging circumstances. Remember who you are and what purpose you serve.

How can you remain focused on the eternal picture?

A NEW COMMANDMENT

"I give you a new command; Love one another. Just as I have loved you, you are also to love one another. By this everyone will know that you are my disciples, if you love one another."

JOHN 13:34-35 CSB

If love is your default posture, you'll be properly following the commandment Jesus gave. If you love others on your own strength, you'll fall short. Love for others becomes a signpost of your commitment to Christ, and it is easier when you're filled with the Father's love for you. His love fills in the gaps when your best efforts fail.

Do you seek to be filled with the Father's love when it's a challenge to love others?

SAFE AND SECURE

The Spirit is God's guarantee that he will give us the inheritance he promised
and that he has purchased us to be his own people.

EPHESIANS 1:14 NLT

Do you ever feel a bit lost in your journey? You get caught up in the busyness
of life, invest in various tasks, roles, and relationships, and then forget your
greater identity in Christ. But here's the truth: you are not truly lost. God has
placed a secure gift within you—the Holy Spirit. He resides in your heart while
he transforms and equips you. He serves as a reminder that you belong to God.

Is God's Spirit speaking to your spirit today?

TO ALL PEOPLE

To the weak I became weak, that I might win the weak. I have become all things to all people, that by all means I might save some. I do it all for the sake of the gospel, that I may share with them in its blessings.

1 CORINTHIANS 9:22-23 ESV

Strong, lasting relationships are built when you celebrate uniqueness and commonality. The needs, struggles, and joys of others miraculously become your needs, struggles, and joys. When people see your willingness to enter their world for the sake of the gospel, doors are opened, walls come down, and people take a step closer to Christ and his kingdom.

How can you reach out to people in need?

NEEDING MORE

He is so rich in kindness and grace that he purchased our freedom
with the blood of his Son and forgave our sins.
EPHESIANS 1:7 NLT

Do you ever wish you had more to offer? You maybe find yourself limited in
your abilities or productivity levels, but what if you had another source to
tap into? God is rich in kindness and grace. While you have limitations in
your kindness and grace, your heavenly Father possesses an immeasurable
abundance that he is willing to share with you.

If you run out kindness and grace, do you remember God's limitless resources?

GROWTH

We can all draw close to him with the veil removed from our faces.
And with no veil we all become like mirrors who brightly reflect
the glory of the Lord Jesus.
2 CORINTHIANS 3:18 TPT

Unlike your body, your spirit doesn't stop growing. And while your body deteriorates, your spirit is constantly being transformed into God's image. You aren't ever fully formed in your spirit. You give others a glimpse of God's glory when your body breaks down, but your spirit builds up.

Are you willing to be transformed from one level of glory to another?

BELONGING

God decided in advance to adopt us into his own family
by bringing us to himself through Jesus Christ.
This is what he wanted to do, and it gave him great pleasure.

EPHESIANS 1:5 NLT

You may not have received gifts from your earthly dad, but your Father in heaven certainly has gifts for you. Giving to you brings him great pleasure. God's gift in this verse is that of belonging to his own family as his own child. One of the most precious gifts you can give to those around us is your time, your attention, and the good news of belonging.

How has God's generosity inspired you to be more generous?

GOD'S GRACE

God saved you by his grace when you believed.
And you can't take credit for this; it is a gift from God.
EPHESIANS 2:8 NLT

You diminish the work on the cross if you think grace is awarded because of your works. You cannot truly receive grace if you believe it is owed to you. When you understand that grace is a gift from God and you did nothing to earn it, you can give it away freely. When you extend grace to others, they walk away with a clearer understanding of the love Christ has for them.

Are your heart and hands open to freely receive and give the gift of grace?

IN MY PLACE

God made him who had no sin to be sin for us,
so that in him we might become the righteousness of God.
2 CORINTHIANS 5:21 NIV

Have you ever faced a messy task? You likely ended up getting messy in the process. Paul explained the incredible work of Christ on your behalf: Jesus entered into your messy life and took all your mess upon himself. Through this exchange, you are made clean, pure, perfect, and holy. Christ's sacrifice on the cross allows you to stand completely righteous before God. Your mess became his, and his perfection became yours.

Can you place your messy life in the capable hands of God?

PURPOSE

We are God's masterpiece. He has created us anew in Christ Jesus,
so we can do the good things he planned for us long ago.
EPHESIANS 2:10 NLT

Your life was created with intention and purpose by the hands of God. You are like no other because you're uniquely equipped to do the work God prepared you to do. Crafting your history, weaving in your gifts, and determining your future, God continues to mold you for his will. He wants to use you to bring life to those around you and to encourage those under your care.

Are your open eyes to see what makes you unique?

IMITATE CHRIST

Be imitators of me, as I am of Christ.
1 CORINTHIANS 11:1 ESV

Have you ever had that eerie feeling of being watched? As a Christian, you are! It might be your curious neighbor, your vigilant boss, or your children. Actively observe and imitate Paul's life in Christ. He was committed to following Jesus and living transparently so others could see and follow his example. Let your faith shine in a way that others can see and imitate you.

How do you imitate Christ?

TRUE POWER

Being found in appearance as a man,
he humbled himself by becoming obedient to death—
even death on a cross!

PHILIPPIANS 2:8 NIV

No matter how high you climb up the ladder of success, you will never have the nature of God. It is an honor to have a high position, but the challenge is in how you use that power. A spirit of humility allows you to use your position to serve others. Jesus relentlessly pursued humility. It led him beyond serving others and took him to the cross.

Are you currently pursuing a path of humility in Christ?

WANDERING SOUL

All of us, like sheep, have strayed away.
We have left God's paths to follow our own.
Yet the LORD laid on him the sins of us all.
ISAIAH 53:6 NLT

You know your own waywardness by simply looking into your heart. Wandering off course is common in anyone's journey with Christ. Isaiah likened it to being a sheep, but also reminded leaders they're no different from those they shepherd. Take heart! No matter how often you stray, through Christ's power, you can be redeemed and find your way back to the flock.

Are you following your Shepherd, trusting his path rather than your own?

FOCUS

Whatever is true, whatever is noble, whatever is right, whatever is pure,
whatever is lovely, whatever is admirable—if anything is excellent or
praiseworthy—think about such things.
PHILIPPIANS 4:8 NIV

The way you think shapes what you observe. The posture of your mind
determines how you experience life. If you're constantly thinking about what
can go wrong, you'll see shortfalls. But if you shift your focus, you will see
beauty. When you focus on what is true, noble, right, pure, lovely, admirable,
excellent, and praiseworthy, you will see the goodness more clearly.

Do you see the benefits in purposefully shifting your focus?

LIGHT SHINES

The people walking in darkness have seen a great light;
a light has dawned on those living in the land of darkness.
ISAIAH 9:2 CSB

Trusting God supersedes common sense. He calls you to trust him radically and deeply even when it defies logic. Faith is trusting God now; hope is trusting him into the future. If you're lost on a road trip, a map will guide you. Jesus illuminates the path for the lost and leads with his perfect plan. Common sense says, "Figure it out," but Jesus says, "I am the light of the world."

Is the light of Christ shining in your heart today?

VISION

These all died in faith, not having received the things promised,
but having seen them and greeted them from afar.
HEBREWS 11:13 ESV

Hebrews tells of the faithful who did not receive the things promised. They
did not see their vision fulfilled, but their lives were not wasted. If your
dreams are unfulfilled, you might think that your pursuit was for nothing.
But if the dream is secondary to the pursuit, you still win. If the pursuit of
your vision is of primary importance, your work in the pursuit validates you
for greater purposes.

Are you in pursuit of something that may or may not come to fruition?

FIND HOPE AGAIN

Those who sow with tears will reap with songs of joy.
Those who go out weeping, carrying seed to sow,
will return with songs of joy, carrying sheaves with them.
PSALM 126:5-6 NIV

God takes his time to accomplish his work; it can be frustrating. But remember, he is intentional and gracious when transforming your life, and his timing is perfect. Everything has a season. God's deep transformation requires a spiritual miracle. Though tears may be sown, they will yield joyful fruit at harvest time. Trust God's timing. You will have both change and joy.

Do you trust God's timing with the transformational work he's doing in you?

SHEPHERDING

Care for the flock that God has entrusted to you. Watch over it willingly, not grudgingly—not for what you will get out of it, but because you are eager to serve God.
1 PETER 5:2 NLT

Leaders have been given a responsibility to nurture, protect, and care for a flock, but there is freedom knowing that flock is ultimately his. When leaders prioritize their flock, the responsibility can be overwhelming. If their priority is God, they trust him to fill in where they fall short. If you are in a position of leadership, trust the Shepherd to help you care for your flock.

How can you lead others in a way that prioritizes God?

LAUGH AGAIN

Our mouths were filled with laughter,
our tongues with songs of joy.
PSALM 126:2 NIV

When was the last time you laughed because of the immense love of Christ? Laughter is a testament to God's transformative work in you. The psalmist declared that even nations would recognize God's goodness when they witnessed your contagious joy. Imagine the impact you can have on your community through the power of laughter.

Does the power of God's love present itself as joy in your life?

GOSPEL MESSENGERS

How beautiful on the mountains
are the feet of the messenger who brings good news.
ISAIAH 52:7 NLT

You may think missionaries serve in far-off lands. When you walk across the street and share your faith with the neighbors, you are accomplishing the same goal as the missionaries who work around the globe. Your calling to share the gospel with those around you is not less noble or important than that of people serving in other countries.

How can you be a messenger of the gospel in your neighborhood this week?

DREAM AGAIN

When the LORD restored the fortunes of Zion,
we were like those who dreamed.
PSALM 126:1 NIV

The challenging seasons in life can steal your dreams and leave you feeling deflated and bereft of passion. But the psalmist says that in the Lord, it's never too late to dream. After years of captivity, God freed his people and allowed them to return home to recapture their dreams. A new season presents an opportunity to rediscover old dreams and to ask God for new ones.

In this season of your life, have you asked God to allow you to dream again?

CEASE STRIVING

"Surrender your anxiety!
Be still and realize that I am God."
PSALM 46:10 TPT

Christian men are constantly being told to work harder, love better. But to cease striving and to know that God is God speaks to the heart. There is nothing your striving can change. Be confident that God is seated on his throne. Sometimes you need to step back from your striving to realize that.

Can you cease striving sometimes to simply contemplate God on his throne?

CONFIDENCE

This is the confidence that we have toward him,
that if we ask anything according to his will he hears us.
1 JOHN 5:14 ESV

The man of God embodies a quiet and genuine confidence. You're called to boldly approach God's presence and pray with unwavering confidence. When you pray confidently, you enter the grandest arena—the heavenly throne room. As God's child, you know he hears you. Be a man of true confidence through your demeanor and your prayers.

Do you pray boldly in faith, knowing that God hears you and answers?

DISCIPLESHIP

It is the greatest joy of my life to hear that my children
are consistently living their lives in the ways of truth!
3 JOHN 1:4 TPT

Few things will bring you more joy than when you excel. As a believer, achieving a relationship with God is primary; it is far more important than any other skill or accomplishment. You can't will yourself to follow Jesus, but you can increase your chances of success by exposing yourself to God's Word, seeking friendships with other Christians, and getting connected to a church.

Do you have friends who follow Christ?

TRANSFORMATIVE LOVE

There is no fear in love, but perfect love casts out fear. For fear has to do with punishment, and whoever fears has not been perfected in love.

1 JOHN 4:18 ESV

You are wired to respond to others based on how they treat you. But with Christ in you, you love even those who don't love you first. This transformative love grants you fearlessness; it empowers you to face everyday challenges. Just like a father fearlessly rushes into a burning house to save his child, God's love in you surpasses any fear you may encounter.

Have you embraced a fearless life by remembering that God's love is greater than any judgment?

FOCUS ON JESUS

Because his heart was focused on the joy of knowing that you would be his,
he endured the agony of the cross and conquered its humiliation, and now
sits exalted at the right hand of the throne of God!
HEBREWS 12:2 TPT

Distractions—job, family, friends, hobbies—are fighting for your attention.
The only way life gets easier is if you're following the guiding light of the one
who has perfect focus—Jesus Christ. If you fix your eyes on him, he will lead
you through the storms and bring clarity to your path.

Are your eyes fixed on Jesus, or are you more focused on worries you can't see?

CHANNEL OF LOVE

Beloved, if God so loved us,
we also ought to love one another.
1 JOHN 4:11 ESV

Love is easy to talk about but difficult to practice. Immerse yourself in God's love through his Word and radiate it to others. You're called to be a channel of God's grace. By embodying his love, you become a conduit to those around you. Love surpasses theory; it's about meeting people's needs. When you do, you become a vessel of God's love, impacting others with his grace.

Can people see the love of Christ in you?

REJOICING

He will take great delight in you;
in his love he will no longer rebuke you,
but will rejoice over you with singing.
ZEPHANIAH 3:17 NIV

Parents often say a prayer or sing a lullaby while tucking in their children, and the kids love it! Many parents don't feel they deserve the absolute devotion of their kids; it's a great picture of how your heavenly Father views you. He lovingly sings over you.

Are you encouraged in your relationship with God by this thought?

OVERCOME

Little children, you are from God and have overcome them,
for he who is in you is greater than he who is in the world.
1 JOHN 4:4 ESV

As a believer, overcoming is inherent. You overcome by persevering in faith, rejecting fear, and obeying even when others don't. You overcome when you remember that the Jesus within you is greater than any worldly force. Victory is assured when you abide in Christ.

How does knowing the truth about Christ's greatness help you overcome any situation you are facing?

MODELING

Brothers, join in imitating me, and keep your eyes on those who walk
according to the example you have in us.
PHILIPPIANS 3:17 ESV

Do you know someone worth following? Are you close to other men who
love Jesus and live for him? Paul said it simply: Follow their example. Would
you be proud to have other men imitate you and watch and learn from you to
be more like Christ? There are plenty of examples not worth following in the
world. You have an opportunity to set an example worthy of being followed.

Who in your life sets a good example?

SHOWING GOD'S LOVE

Little children, let us not love in word
or talk but in deed and in truth.
1 JOHN 3:18 ESV

Love is more than a duty; it helps you discover your true purpose as a child of God. Your identity precedes your actions. Love flows through you because of Christ. You may encounter people you dislike for various reasons, yet love goes beyond personal preferences. It is not just an idea or sentiment; it requires action.

Who will you show God's love to today?

APPROVAL

Am I now trying to win the approval of human beings, or of God?
Or am I trying to please people? If I were still trying to please people,
I would not be a servant of Christ.
GALATIANS 1:10 NIV

It's understandable that you want people to approve of you, but as a servant of Christ you must take a different path. You will only experience true peace when it is God's approval that you pursue. The things God approves of often run contrary to the ways of this world. As you place God's opinion above the opinions of those around you, he will continue to draw you closer.

How can you pursue God's approval above that of men?

A GREAT FUTURE

Beloved, we are God's children now, and what we will be has not yet appeared; but we know that when he appears we shall be like him, because we shall see him as he is.

1 JOHN 3:2 ESV

You are undoubtedly eagerly awaiting the return of Jesus. He will come at the appointed time, after the message reaches all nations. His return will bring a remarkable transformation. Through Christ, you have already experienced a change in your nature, an awareness of sin, and a desire to live for God. His return will complete this change because you are destined for glory.

Do you take comfort in knowing that God has a great future planned for you?

ARTICULATE THANKFULNESS

I will give thank the LORD with all my heart;
I will declare all your wondrous works.
PSALM 9:1 CSB

You may find it difficult to articulate the things you're thankful for. It's not that you aren't thankful; it's just not always easy to verbalize it. Take some time today to write down things you're grateful for no matter how big or small they are. You'll be surprised at all you have to be thankful for.

What do you do to cultivate a grateful heart?

FAMILY OF GOD

See what kind of love the Father has given to us, that we should be called children of God; and so we are. The reason why the world does not know us is that it did not know him.

1 JOHN 3:1 ESV

As a believer in the redeeming grace of Christ, you are part of God's family. As God's child, you are forgiven, and you have his presence forever with you in your heart. You hold a unique and secure position as an heir, boldly approaching your Father in prayer and experiencing his love daily. You are embraced and cherished, a valued member of God's family.

How do you intend to live with joy and honor, representing the family of God?

SELF-CONTROL

I do not run aimlessly; I do not box as one beating the air. But I discipline my body and keep it under control, lest after preaching to others I myself should be disqualified.

1 CORINTHIANS 9:26-27 ESV

Imagine a runner who drags his feet, gets distracted by the crowd, and stops to check his phone. Then picture a focused runner with eyes fixed. He hears the crowd, but he keeps moving forward, and he checks his watch only to ensure he's running at the right pace. Are you focused or aimless? Are you running with a plan, or are you making things up as you go?

How can you discipline yourself to stay focused during your race?

STEADFAST

Let what you heard from the beginning abide in you.
If what you heard from the beginning abides in you,
then you too will abide in the Son and in the Father.
1 JOHN 2:24 ESV

When replacing a light fixture, the grounding wire is crucial. It prevents you from becoming an electrical conductor and getting shocked. When unexpected events happen, you need to be grounded. As you get older things may become unclear, but remembering your experiences in Jesus will keep you from being shaken during life's storms.

Is Jesus your grounding wire?

SPEAK UP

Speak up for those who cannot speak for themselves;
ensure justice for those being crushed.
PROVERBS 31:8 NLT

It's your responsibility as a believer to speak for those who cannot speak for themselves. The verse above describes what King Lemuel learned from his mother. He was in a position of power, and he wisely gave his mother's words credence as he taught others. Are you treating people properly and speaking for those who cannot speak for themselves? The way you live today will influence others around you.

Do these words from King Lemuel influence your life principles?

HIGHER WISDOM

If anyone longs to be wise, ask God for wisdom and he will give it! He won't see your lack of wisdom as an opportunity to scold you over your failures but he will overwhelm your failures with his generous grace.

JAMES 1:5 TPT

King Solomon prayed to God for one thing: wisdom. God was pleased with his request, so he rewarded him with unparalleled discernment and added riches and honor. In your own trials, human understanding falls short. You may lack answers or resources, your plans fail, and conflicts arise. Thankfully, God encourages you to ask for wisdom and promises to give generously.

Have you accepted God's help to overcome challenges?

QUICK TO LISTEN

Let every man be quick to hear,
slow to speak, slow to anger.
JAMES 1:19 ESV

Being quick to hear, slow to speak, and slow to anger is not natural. Your instincts are to take control and fix things. You offer advice or criticism and jump to conclusions, but this leads to fighting, bitterness, and grudges. James' words are a reminder of the importance of listening first. When you do, you show concern for others, and you are reminded that you're not the expert.

How do you listen for the quiet voice of God?

MENTORING

Remember your leaders, who have spoken God's word to you.
As you carefully observe the outcome of their lives, imitate their faith.
HEBREWS 13:7 CSB

You are never alone. Growth comes from observing people and having some of them guide you. Hebrews 11 displays courageous heroes from the Bible who stood firm in their faith. Their decision-making, love, prayers, financial decisions, and conflict resolution can inspire you to follow God and grow stronger in your faith.

How do other godly men encourage you in your faith journey?

PRAYER

Confess your sins to each other and pray for each other so that you may be
healed. The prayer of a righteous person is powerful and effective.
JAMES 5:16 NIV

Jumping straight to "the prayer of a righteous person is powerful and
effective," means you'll miss some good stuff! James gives a reminder of the
importance of confessing sins to one another. That's difficult. Confessing your
mistakes is not a form of weakness; it's an example of righteousness.

Do you need to confess anything to a close friend today?

FAITH IN GOD'S PLAN

The power of faith prompted Isaac to impart a blessing to his sons,
Jacob and Esau, concerning their prophetic destinies.
HEBREWS 11:20 TPT

Just as Isaac was called to live by faith, so are you. Isaac understood that the bigger picture belonged to God, and he prioritized his guidance. Similarly, you face situations where God may challenge your plans or desires. Isaac's life exemplified the importance of living by faith, trusting in God's guidance for the future.

Can you think of situations where God asked you to trust him instead of your own plans?

FREEDOM IN CHRIST

I do not do what I want, but I do the very thing I hate.
Wretched man that I am!
ROMANS 7:24 ESV

How many times have you said these same words to yourself? Romans 7 recorded Paul's frustration with his inability to do the right thing. Paul doesn't ask what he needs to do or how he can try harder; he realized that there wasn't anything he could do on his own. You're not good enough to overcome your sin on your own, but Jesus won that battle for you. Accept all he has done for you and walk in victory through him.

Do you find yourself frustrated when you can't seem to do the right thing?

LIVING BY FAITH

Without faith it is impossible to please him, for whoever would draw near to God must believe that he exists and that he rewards those who seek him.
HEBREWS 11:6 ESV

Living by faith is challenging because it goes against all that is normal in the world. True faith is not blind; it is grounded in real evidence which many people reject without investigating. This evidence includes Jesus' resurrection and the existence of a loving God. By embracing faith, you tap into God's story, which is more real than the natural world.

Has God's story become your story?

CONFIDENCE IN GOD

Great is our LORD, and mighty in power;
His understanding is infinite.
PSALM 147:5 NKJV

God's understanding is infinite. The previous verse says that he even knows the number of stars in the sky and calls them by name. There is nothing that is beyond God's comprehension. There's a whole list of qualities that you probably ascribe to God, but do you know about his understanding? He knows you intimately.

How can you lean into God's understanding today?

ARMOR AND STRENGTH

Be strong in the Lord and in the strength of his might. Put on the whole armor of God, that you may be able to stand against the schemes of the devil.
EPHESIANS 6:10-11 ESV

At some point, you discover that life resembles a battleground rather than a playground. You face tests, tough times, and attacks. Battle-time living requires vigilance, strategy, and focus. You recognize false cultural ideas which challenge your values. You acknowledge the potential for your old nature to resist God's ways. Thankfully, God equips you for this battle with spiritual armor, and he sent you a champion in Jesus Christ.

How is God showing his strength in your life today?

PASSION

I am not ashamed of the Good News, because it is the power God uses to save everyone who believes—to save the Jews first, and then to save non-Jews.
ROMANS 1:16 NCV

You probably have things you're passionate about that you wouldn't be ashamed of. Do you feel the same way about the gospel? Is it as easy for you to share what God has accomplished in your life as it is to talk about the stats from last night's game? The gospel is God's power for salvation for all who believe! Proudly share your story of what the gospel has done for you.

Do you speak unashamedly about the gospel?

POWER

Be filled with the Spirit, addressing one another in psalms and hymns and spiritual songs, singing and making melody to the Lord with your heart, giving thanks always and for everything to God the Father in the name of our Lord Jesus Christ, submitting to one another out of reverence for Christ.
EPHESIANS 5:18-21 ESV

When you surrender your will to God, the Holy Spirit takes control and guides you. If there are conflicts in your relationships, a stagnant prayer life, struggles between your old and new self, or little evidence of the fruit of the Spirit in your life, spend more time in prayer.

Have you asked God to fill you with the Holy Spirit?

MENTORSHIP

We loved you so much that we shared with you
not only God's Good News but our own lives, too.
1 THESSALONIANS 2:8 NLT

Consider the people who have spiritually invested the most in you. When you share your life with someone, it builds trust. When you invite people into your day, they get to observe you living the truth. By sharing the good news and your own life, you're showing them that you truly love them.

Are you prepared to be a mentor?

WALKING IN LOVE

Be imitators of God, as beloved children. And walk in love, as Christ loved us and gave himself up for us, a fragrant offering and sacrifice to God.
EPHESIANS 5:1-2 ESV

You are called to imitate God! It may sound impossible, but you are called to imitate God as a beloved child. That reveals both the reason and the character behind your call. As God's child, you naturally resemble him, just as your voice, smile, walk, or wit may resemble your dad's. You resemble God in how you love, and the love of Jesus working through you is what makes that possible.

Do you try to imitate God?

LEADERSHIP

"As for me and my family,
we will worship the LORD."
JOSHUA 24:15 CSB

There are a lot of things over which you won't have any control. That's scary. You want to ensure your loved ones have a safe place to live. Much of the world has turned its back on God. You don't have control over the world, the country, or even your own community, but you do have some control over your own home. Commit to leading the way by serving the Lord at home.

Do you desire to serve the Lord in your home?

RECREATED

You are no longer strangers and aliens, but you are fellow citizens with the saints and members of the household of God, built on the foundation of the apostles and prophets, Christ Jesus himself being the cornerstone.

EPHESIANS 2:19-20 ESV

You have been recreated as a fellow citizen and member of God's own family. Old restrictions no longer apply. You are a holy temple where God's Spirit resides. Your past no longer defines you, and you are not controlled by old habits, memories, or fears. Because you have experienced forgiveness, you forgive. You have been truly and wonderfully recreated.

Do you thank God for being recreated?

FATHERHOOD

"Our Father in heaven,
may your name be kept holy."
MATTHEW 6:9 NLT

When teaching his disciples to pray, Jesus addressed God as Father, creating a beautiful picture of intimacy. Your earthly father is intended to model your relationship with God, although all will fall short, and some fathers provide better examples than others. What have you learned about your relationship with God through your experiences with your father?

Does or did your earthly father give you insight into God the Father?

VISIONARY PRAYER

I pray that the eyes of your heart may be enlightened in order that you may know the hope to which he has called you, the riches of his glorious inheritance in his holy people, and his incomparably great power for us who believe.
EPHESIANS 1:18-19 NIV

Paul prayed for a God-shaped vision; to see God's hope, riches, and power available to all believers. This hope trusts in God's promise of your inheritance. The vision includes the same power that raised Jesus from the dead. It empowers you to live with authority, knowing that Jesus in you is greater than anything in the world.

Do you have a God-shaped vision of hope, riches, and power?

BUILDING A FOUNDATION

Start children off on the way they should go,
and even when they are old they will not turn from it.
PROVERBS 22:6 NIV

Even if your parents did everything right in raising you, they are not the
ones who ultimately mold and change your heart. That is the work of your
heavenly Father. Their job was to start you off on the way you should go. Your
parents' window of influence in your life is limited, but God's work is over
your eternal life.

Will you continue to build on the Godly foundation laid in your life?

TIME TO WORSHIP

Early the next morning they arose and worshiped before the LORD
and then went back to their home at Ramah.

1 SAMUEL 1:19 NIV

Worship is important to God. He loves to hear from you. Consistently
spending time with him sets the spiritual tone for the week. Wake up and
spend a moment in his presence. It's wonderful to do that before the day
vies for your attention. When you make worship a priority, you will start to
anticipate God's voice and his will.

Is worship a priority in your life?

MOTIVATION

We always thank God for all of you and continually mention you in our prayers. We remember before our God and Father your work produced by faith, your labor prompted by love, and your endurance inspired by hope in our Lord Jesus Christ.
1 THESSALONIANS 1:2-3 NIV

Paul thanked God for the believers in Thessalonica: for work produced by faith, labor prompted by love, and endurance inspired by hope in the Lord. When you allow your relationship with Christ to impact you, your motivation changes. You'll work even when it's difficult because of your hope in eternity.

Is your life filled with faith, hope, and love, or marked by duty and obligation?

THE LORD'S PRAYER

"Give us this day our daily bread, and forgive us our debts, as we also have forgiven our debtors. And lead us not into temptation, but deliver us from evil."
MATTHEW 6:11-13 ESV

When you pray, you are aligning your heart with God's heart by seeking his plans and his kingdom. Your humble prayers express your dependence on God and a desire for his direction in your day. Effective prayer needs your focus; it connects you to God's heart and invites his involvement in your life.

Do you pray specifically for provision, forgiveness, and deliverance?

ACCESS TO GOD

In Christ we can come before God with freedom and without fear.
We can do this through faith in Christ.
EPHESIANS 3:12 NCV

How quickly you can forget that you have direct access to God, the Creator of the universe! He gladly welcomes you into his presence because of what Jesus accomplished for you on the cross. Are you apprehensive about speaking to God? Do you forget that he listens? Because of your relationship with Jesus, you can boldly approach him any time or place.

Do you enjoy talking to God?

FEAR

"I, I am he who comforts you; who are you that you are afraid of man who dies, of the son of man who is made like grass, and have forgotten the LORD, your Maker, who stretched out the heavens and laid the foundations of the earth, and you fear continually all the day because of the wrath of the oppressor."

ISAIAH 51:12-13 ESV

Fear can hinder you from fulfilling God's intentions for your life. Israel faced defeat, but King Hezekiah trusted God. To conquer the fear of man, you need a greater fear of the Almighty God. When you fear him, there is no need to fear anything else. The power of God defends and protects you.

Do you find yourself being distracted from God when you fear people?

EFFECTIVE MINISTRY

Make every effort to add to your faith goodness; and to goodness,
knowledge; and to knowledge, self-control; and to self-control, perseverance;
and to perseverance, godliness; and to godliness, mutual affection; and to
mutual affection, love.

2 PETER 1:5-7 NIV

You probably want to be the best man you can be. In the verses above, Peter lists eight characteristics of an effective person. While you may see them as a to-do list, the traits will never be fully developed. You will spend a lifetime growing.

Do you have more of these qualities in your life today than you did last year?

FEAR OR TRUST

"The LORD is on my side; I will not fear.
What can man do to me?"
PSALM 118:6 ESV

Fear affects many different areas of life. You may fear illness, financial instability, or a natural disaster. You may struggle with how you handle fear. It's possible that you perceive it as a sign of weakness, so you strive to avoid it. You will inevitably face fearful situations. The Bible says not to fear because God provides an antidote: trust in him.

Do you trust your heavenly Father more than you fear anything else?

FAITHFULNESS

You must honor the LORD and truly serve him with all your heart.
Remember the wonderful things he did for you!

1 SAMUEL 12:24 NCV

Find time today to list some of the great things God is doing. Don't rush. Carefully consider his greatness. You are called to fear the Lord and worship him faithfully. This becomes easier when you're thinking about all the great things he is doing. As you lead in your various realms of influence, allow your thankfulness to God to cause you to be a man who fears and worships him with all your heart.

When was the last time you considered the blessings of God?

PREPARING FOR BLESSING

Know that the LORD, he is God!
It is he who made us, and we are his;
we are his people, and the sheep of his pasture.
PSALM 100:3 ESV

To experience God's blessing, you must understand three essential truths: know who God is, recognize that it is he who created you, and understand who leads you. Like a sheep, you are guided by a Good Shepherd who knows you, provides for you, and protects you. This Shepherd will ultimately lead you to your eternal home in heaven.

Do you want to know more about God, so you understand yourself better?

PERSONAL DEVOTION

You sinners, clean sin out of your lives. You who are trying to follow God
and the world at the same time, make your thinking pure.

JAMES 4:8 NCV

There's only room for one leader in your life. You have to choose. God gives
you the ability to stand against the devil's temptations. You are no longer
controlled by the power of sin. When you stand against the devil's schemes
and draw near to God, not only will he draw near to you, but the devil will
become less and less powerful.

As you draw nearer to God, do you observe temptations falling away?

EXPERIENCE

Drink deeply of the pleasures of this God.
Experience for yourself the joyous mercies he gives
to all who turn to hide themselves in him.
PSALM 34:8 TPT

Finding God's presence and hearing his voice requires time and practice. When you're desperate, God will reveal himself and rescue you, but isn't always immediate. As you travel life's path, you will experience his goodness. Those moments ground your growing faith, which replaces fear with reverence and frees you from your everyday worries. True refuge lies in God alone.

Are you ready to embark on a new adventure to see God work in your life?

LOVING GOD

Loving God means keeping his commandments,
and his commandments are not burdensome.
1 JOHN 5:3 NLT

The best way for children to show their love for their parents is to do what they've asked of them. It's no different for you demonstrating your love for God. You display your love for him not just through the words you say to him but also by the way you live your life. Actions truly do speak louder than words.

How are you showing your love for your heavenly Father today?

DELIVERANCE

I sought the LORD, and he answered me
and delivered me from all my fears.
PSALM 34:4 ESV

David's deliverance from his fears began by seeking the Lord. God saved him from those fears and other trouble besides. You may be chasing ideal circumstances, trying to hedge against future challenges, or get a better position at your job. Possessions and circumstances never satisfy. As you seek the Lord, listen to his voice, and find contentment in his answers, you'll experience profound joy.

Do you seek the Lord and listen to his answers?

UNIQUELY GIFTED

As each has received a gift, use it to serve one another,
as good stewards of God's varied grace.
1 PETER 4:10 ESV

God has uniquely gifted each of his children with talents and abilities. Can you identify how the people around you are gifted? God has not gifted you uniquely for your own benefit. You are called to use your gifts to serve and help others. As you do, you'll discover that people are stronger when they use their gifts in conjunction with each other.

Have you discerned what your gifts are?

PRAISE

I will bless the LORD at all times;
his praise shall continually be in my mouth.
PSALM 34:1 ESV

David did not consider praise to simply be a compliment to God. It was an overflow of joy from a life enriched by him. Each person expresses their praises differently; some are loud and spontaneous; some are quiet and steady. Unlike selfish pleasure which diminishes over time, praising God expands your capacity for joy and increases your delight in him.

Have you praised God today?

DECISION TO ENGAGE

"Eli, Eli, lema sabachthani?" (which means
"My God, my God, why have you forsaken me?"
MATTHEW 27:46 NIV

The Bible teaches that worship is a decision to engage with God; it's an offering with a cost. Mission and worship are inseparable. Perhaps the best demonstration was on Calvary's cross. Jesus engaged in the mission of God as the bloodied, beaten Savior, and he lifted his voice to worship his Father. The man, Jesus, hanging on a cross, found within his heart a desire to sing praises to God.

Do you worship your Father when you're bloodied and beaten?

SIGHT OF VISION

The LORD opened the eyes of the young man, and he saw. And behold, the mountain was full of horses and chariots of fire all around Elisha.
2 KINGS 6:17 NKJV

Helen Keller once said, "Being born without vision is worse than being born without sight." Elisha and his servant experienced this noteworthy difference. The servant saw only the enemy army which caused him to despair, but Elisha prayed for him to see God's work, and his eyes were opened. You need vision to understand God's plans. Disappointments may surround you, but with God, there is no reason to fear.

Have you prayed lately for God's vision so you can really see?

OUR WORTH

As a prisoner for the Lord, then, I urge you to live a life
worthy of the calling you have received.
EPHESIANS 4:1 NIV

You have received the high calling of being a child of God; you should be living in a way worthy of this calling. Do the words *humble, gentle,* and *patient* describe you? These are the qualities that you should aspire to. Allow these traits to motivate you to a higher standard of character, not so you can earn God's favor, but so you can live the way God already sees you.

Do you seek your worth in the presence and character of God?

VICTORY

"One of you routs a thousand, because the LORD your God fights for you, just as he promised. So be very careful to love the LORD your God."
JOSHUA 23:10-11 NIV

When Joshua was old, he reflected on his battles and God's faithfulness throughout the move into the Promised Land. Today, God also fights for you. You face enemies of sin, external challenges, and pressures from and on your loved ones. But when God is on your side, incredible things happen. With his strength, you can conquer any adversity.

Do you remember God in your victories?

ATTITUDE

Rejoice in the Lord always; again I will say, rejoice.
Let your reasonableness be known to everyone. The Lord is at hand.
PHILIPPIANS 4:4-5 ESV

It's easy to rejoice when things are going well, but how can you rejoice when things are tough? Paul wrote these words while sitting in a prison cell. He knew the constant, dependable presence of the Lord. You can rejoice in knowing that God is aware of your specific circumstances, and he is with you. Each new day, adopt an attitude that rejoices in the Lord at all times.

Can you acknowledge the Lord's presence with you in each moment?

SUCCESS

"This Book of the Law shall not depart from your mouth, but you shall meditate in it day and night, that you may observe to do according to all that is written in it."

JOSHUA 1:8 NKJV

When God calls you, he empowers you and guarantees your success for his purposes. He provides a clear roadmap. Just as Joshua meditated on the Word of God as he led Israel's armies, you will find victory by meditating on God's powerful, written Word. Your success is directly tied to how much God's Word influences your thoughts and your actions each day.

Do you meditate on the Word day and night?

GODLINESS

Man of God, flee from all this, and pursue righteousness, godliness, faith, love, endurance and gentleness. Fight the good fight of the faith.

1 TIMOTHY 6:11-12 NIV

Being a child of God requires action; you can't just expect things to happen. You've been called to a high standard of living which can only be realized with a commitment to action. Flee from the evil around you and pursue that which is good. Be willing to fight for your faith. Remember the destination is eternal life with Christ.

Are you prepared to flee, pursue, fight, and take hold?

STRONG AND BRAVE

"Joshua, be strong and brave! You must lead these people so they can take the land that I promised their fathers I would give them."
JOSHUA 1:6 NCV

Joshua led over six hundred thousand people into a land filled with enemies and peril. He was called to be strong, which was based on both God's promise to be with him and his own obedience to God's commands. God is calling you to be strong today. Like Joshua, your success depends on the same two things: God's promise to be with you and your obedience to God.

When a conditional promise is made by God, are you willing to hold up your end?

STRENGTH IN WEAKNESS

"My grace is sufficient for you, for my power is made perfect in weakness."
Therefore I will boast all the more gladly of my weaknesses, so that the
power of Christ may rest upon me.

2 CORINTHIANS 12:9 ESV

It's difficult to admit your weaknesses. You will be the best man and leader for
God's kingdom when you allow God's grace and power to be evident in your
life. You are strongest when you live dependently upon God's work in your
life. Make room for God's power by admitting to your weaknesses.

How are you honest with the Lord about your shortcomings?

MERCY AND GRACE

"The LORD—the LORD is a compassionate and gracious God,
slow to anger and abounding in faithful love and truth,
maintaining faithful love to a thousand generations."
EXODUS 34:6-7 CSB

You may desire a personal encounter with God. Though human limitations prevent you from fully perceiving his glory and magnificence, God still orchestrates extraordinary moments when you can experience his wonder. Despite the righteous standards and lingering effects of sin, God's grace extends for a thousand generations, encompassing an amazing legacy.

How have you seen the Father's compassion and mercy?

THANKFULNESS

Oh give thanks to the LORD;
call upon his name;
make known his deeds among the peoples!
PSALM 105:1 ESV

One of the first things you are taught to say is, "Thank you." Children and adults send thank-you notes for gifts, thank coaches and teachers, and say grace before a meal. In God, there is so much to be thankful for. This verse instructs believers to not just say thank you to God for all that he has done, but also to tell others. Make known his deeds among the peoples!

How can you share with others what God has done for you?

GUIDANCE

"My presence will go with you, and I will give you rest." And he said to him, "If your presence will not go with me, do not bring us up from here."
EXODUS 33:14-15 ESV

Leading millions of people through a desolate wilderness for forty years was an immense challenge. Most people would find even a short family road trip trying, let alone a forty-year journey! But Moses understood that the essence of life was in having God's presence. That offered guidance, protection, and blessing. God longs to be present with you, bringing rest and peace to your life.

Do you abide in Jesus?

GOD IS GREATER

The foolishness of God is wiser than human wisdom,
and the weakness of God is stronger than human strength.
1 CORINTHIANS 1:25 NIV

God is always greater than humans. Even at your strongest, you won't compare to God. It's encouraging to know that God is not only wise and strong, but he is also on your side. He is equipped and sufficient to help you in every situation. When others come to you for help, you can point them to your wise and wonderful God.

When you reach the limits of your own capabilities, do you remember to ask God for his strength?

COUNTING BLESSINGS

"The blessings of your father are mighty beyond the blessings of my parents, up to the bounties of the everlasting hills. May they be on the head of Joseph, and on the brow of him who was set apart from his brothers."
GENESIS 49:26 ESV

Jacob lived long with a few high points and much conflict. When reunited with Joseph, he called his years few and unpleasant. But years later, he said that God had blessed him. What changed? Jacob saw God's mercies which covered each adversity. You can focus on your disappointments, or you can focus on God's ways of blessing you through them.

Are you grateful when God gives you mercy through your adversities?

THE GOLDEN RULE

"Do to others what you would want them to do to you."
LUKE 6:31 NCV

Sometimes it's the simple things that make the most sense. Do you model the behavior you want to see in others? People may listen to your words, but they're much more likely to follow the behaviors, attitudes, and actions they see modeled by you. Do you treat others as you want to be treated?

Are you tuned in to your behavior so you're aware of how you treat others?

GOD WHO ANSWERS

"Then let us arise and go up to Bethel, so that I may make there an altar to the God who answers me in the day of my distress and has been with me wherever I have gone."

GENESIS 35:3 ESV

Jacob's family was in chaos, and he worried about their safety. God called him back to Bethel, thirty miles south. That was the same place Jacob met God thirty years earlier, and he pledged that the Lord would be his God. When you drift away from God, he calls you back.

Has the Lord brought you back to your original love for him?

RIGHT UNDERSTANDING

"I will never leave you nor forsake you."
HEBREWS 13:5 ESV

God is your creator, provider, sustainer, and defender. When you have a right understanding of who he is, and what he has done, your priorities and values begin to change. Knowing that God has promised to never leave you or forsake you brings great comfort. God has promised to care for you. He will provide everything you need.

Do you trust God as your provider?

PEACE

Laban said, "This heap is a witness between you and me today." Therefore he named it Galeed, and Mizpah, for he said, "The LORD watch between you and me, when we are out of one another's sight."

GENESIS 31:48-49 ESV

Distrust and resentment had grown between Laban and Jacob. Finally, they built a memorial and there both submitted to God. They feared displeasing God more than they disagreed with each other. Sometimes you'll find that conflicts are unavoidable, but like Jacob and Laban, you need to stop the conflict from getting any worse.

Do your disagreements with people get in the way of hearing from God?

GRACE AND FORGIVENESS

Make allowance for each other's faults, and forgive anyone who offends you.
Remember, the Lord forgave you, so you must forgive others.
COLOSSIANS 3:13 NLT

Grace and forgiveness are powerful. They could fix most relationship problems. Extending or requesting forgiveness changes the dynamic of a strained friendship. Relationships can be messy, but if you want others to make allowances for you, you should do the same for them.

Do you extend grace and forgiveness in your relationships?

OUR PROVIDER

"God will provide for himself the lamb for a burnt offering, my son." So they went both of them together. So Abraham called the name of that place, "The LORD will provide"; as it is said to this day, "On the mount of the LORD it shall be provided."

GENESIS 22:8,14 ESV

Abraham took wood to sacrifice his son and went to Moriah on the third day. Moriah is near Calvary where God sacrificed his Son two thousand years later. Moriah, wood, and the third day. The grief in Abraham's heart was felt by the Almighty God, who offered his own Son years later as the final sacrifice.

Do you have the eyes to see God moving in your life?

DELIGHT IN GOD

Take delight in the LORD,
and he will give you your heart's desires.
PSALM 37:4 NLT

When you delight in God, you start to want more of him, and your desires are shaped to align with his. True commitment to God will determine how you see yourself and others. It doesn't make life easier, but it gives you wisdom and grace for life's happenings.

Do you consistently recommit yourself to your relationship with God?

FUEL OF LOVE

We love because he first loved us.
1 JOHN 4:19 ESV

Love in truth finds its energy in the work and person of Jesus Christ. You love the poor because he became poor. You welcome others because you have received the Spirit of adoption. Your forgiveness is rooted in the call of Christ to forgive as he forgave. Christ is the fuel of love that empowers the soul!

Does God's love fuel you so you can love the people in your life?

GOD'S WILL

"For I know the plans I have for you," says the LORD.
"They are plans for good and not for disaster,
to give you a future and a hope."
JEREMIAH 29:11 NLT

This verse can get people excited, but the verse before it is also important.
The Israelites were in captivity for seventy years! The future is bright, but
circumstances don't change overnight. You may want to know the plan before
you are settled, but it includes a process. Trust that God has great plans for
you in that process.

Are you okay with the process even when you're aware of God's plan?

DEBT OF LOVE

Owe no one anything, except to love each other,
for the one who loves another has fulfilled the law.
ROMANS 13:8 ESV

God's display of divine love is a model for you to emulate. You can also pay it forward as an expression of gratitude. Serving in love honors the name that bought you salvation. The Lord himself commissioned you to let your light shine before others, so they are drawn to the Father in heaven.

Does your love and gratitude toward others reflect the love given for you?

REMOVE THE CLUTTER

"Blessed are the poor in spirit,
for theirs is the kingdom of heaven."
MATTHEW 5:3 NIV

When your life is uncluttered, you have a greater awareness of God. When everything is stripped away, a new level of trust in God is experienced. Jesus encourages his followers to be drawn into a deeper level of trust. Consider what you might need to strip away in order to deepen your relationship with God.

How can you model a life of simplicity?

ENDLESS SUPPLY

He who did not spare his own Son but gave him up for us all,
how will he not also with him graciously give us all things?
ROMANS 8:32 ESV

Loneliness and despair can find their way into your life. Rest assured during those seasons that God is always faithful. He is an endless well of life, vitality, and security. When the world strips you of your hope, he is the covering that brings restoration to the soul. You have a heavenly Father who is good to you.

Do you doubt the timely provision of the Lord?

GENEROSITY

"When you give to the needy, do not let your left hand know what your right hand is doing, so that your giving may be in secret. And your Father who sees in secret will reward you."

MATTHEW 6:3-4 NIV

Jesus talked about the rich, the poor, and money a lot. Giving seemed to be a top priority for him. Generosity is easier said than done, and the wallet is often the final thing handed over to Jesus. When you do give, the Father is pleased with you. There's no need to let everyone know. It's your choice to glorify God instead of seeking man's empty praises.

Are you secretly generous somewhere in your life?

COSTLY LOVE

God shows his love for us in that while we were still sinners,
Christ died for us.
ROMANS 5:8 ESV

Love, service, and discipleship without any cost do not reflect gospel-saturated love. As the world continues to fight for convenience, embrace the sacrificial love that is personified in Jesus Christ. Giving of yourself entails posturing your heart in accordance with the Lord to convey the message of the gospel through service to others.

Do you serve others for God's sake or for your own?

MONEY

"Store your treasures in heaven, where moths and rust cannot destroy, and thieves do not break in and steal. Wherever your treasure is, there the desires of your heart will also be."

MATTHEW 6:20-21 NLT

"I have this kind of car." "Oh yeah? I have *that* kind of car." One-upping is almost an art form. It's easy to fall into the trap of wanting all the latest stuff. Jesus warned against this idolatry because he recognized the toll it takes on the heart. It reveals what you really desire and who you really are.

Do you put too much stock in things?

MORE OF HIM

That I may know him and the power of his resurrection,
and may share his sufferings, becoming like him in his death.
PHILIPPIANS 3:10 ESV

Mimicking Jesus may not produce the so-called success that you are looking for, yet reorienting your expectations and redefining advancement might be what's necessary in realizing the biblical definition of success. When you view the world through the gospel lens, you will find that trends do not dictate faithful service to the Lord.

Is your end goal to be more like Jesus?

PROVIDENCE

"Do not worry, saying, 'What shall we eat?' or 'What shall we drink?' or
'What shall we wear?'"
MATTHEW 6:31 NIV

Provision can be one of the most rewarding, yet worrisome, responsibilities
you have. If you think so much about providing for yourself, how much more
does God think about providing for you? It can be daunting, but Jesus' tells
you not to worry. It may not be as you imagined it, but faith allows you to
release your worries so you can trust in God.

Is your daily bread from you or from God?

HEART POSTURE

Do all things without grumbling or disputing.
PHILIPPIANS 2:14 ESV

As a believer in Jesus, posture your heart in a such a manner that you always seek to bring him praise and honor. He says that complaining and arguing is not behavior that he wants his children to emulate. Put on his character and walk in his meekness.

Are you able to do all things without grumbling or disputing?

PERSISTENT PRAYER

"Keep on asking, and you will receive what you ask for. Keep on seeking, and you will find. Keep on knocking, and the door will be opened to you."
MATTHEW 7:7 NLT

Jesus tells you to pray persistently. As you seek God, you will find him. Prayer might seem challenging at times, but as you keep praying, you will grow. What do the people in your life need? What gifts are they developing? Ask God to help them grow. Maybe your time of prayer could include a few minutes of seeking God's voice in silence.

What are you persistently asking God for today?

SUFFERING

It has been granted to you that for the sake of Christ you should not only believe in him but also suffer for his sake.

PHILIPPIANS 1:29 ESV

It's popular to question the Lord's goodness in the middle of suffering. Yet, from a biblical standpoint, suffering is the means by which God conforms you into the image of his Son. When bad things happen in your life, don't ask "Why me?" Instead ask, "What are you teaching me?" You can be assured that he is working for your good.

Do you seek God's glory or your own comfort?

KINGDOM OF GOD

"The Kingdom of Heaven is like a mustard seed planted in a field.
It is the smallest of all seeds, but it becomes the largest of garden plants;
it grows into a tree, and birds come and make nests in its branches."
MATTHEW 13:31-32 NLT

Jesus often talked about the kingdom of God. He compared it to something small and seemingly insignificant, but over time—perhaps a long time—it will grow. In the illustration above, Jesus talks about the kingdom of heaven being a home and a refuge. Small beginnings can lead to places of great refuge and trust.

Are you a safe refuge for others in your life?

MANNER OF LIFE

Let your manner of life be worthy of the gospel of Christ.
PHILIPPIANS 1:27 ESV

Your belief system governs the external expression of your life. Verbal commitments are shallow and meaningless without a consistent response in conduct, commitment, and propriety. The common thread that is produced in your facial expressions communicates the posture of your heart.

Does your manner of life reflect the truth that resides in your heart?

POSSESSIONS

"If you want to be perfect, go and sell all your possessions and give the money
to the poor, and you will have treasure in heaven. Then come, follow me."
MATTHEW 19:21 NLT

In Western culture, consumerism is everything, but Jesus appealed to a
different kind of living. To be perfect, you may have to get rid of stuff, just
as he instructed the rich man. He called his followers to a life that is not
dominated by things. Don't let your heart and head be so cluttered that you
have no room to be mindful of God or people in need.

How can you model simple and generous living?

RIGHTEOUS CHARACTER

May you always be filled with the fruit of your salvation—
the righteous character produced in your life by Jesus Christ—
for this will bring much glory and praise to God.
PHILIPPIANS 1:11 NLT

Though the Lord's commandments are important to the faith, they are not the entry point through which a union with Christ is obtained. When you grasp the truth that your right standing with God is dependent upon Christ's fulfillment of the law, you will walk in humility.

Do you lean into the identity of Jesus Christ to find righteousness?

LEAD THROUGH SERVING

"Whoever wants to become great among you
must serve the rest of you like a servant."
MATTHEW 20:26 NCV

When Jesus spoke to his disciples about leadership, he said the best leaders
serve. As a child, you were served by your parents because you couldn't do
things for yourself. As you grew, you were taught responsibilities, so you
didn't expect to keep being served. To model servant leadership, find ways to
meet the needs of those in your sphere of influence.

Are you willing to lead by getting your hands dirty?

LOVE IS SOMEONE

God is love.
1 JOHN 4:8 ESV

Love is not merely an affection, concept, or devotion. Love is defined in God. Society considers love an emotive principle which is determined by the individual, but the biblical account forges a different reality. Love is unified with truth in the person of Jesus. He is the standard of the power of love.

How can you seek an honest and full definition of love in God?

INVESTMENT

"Well done, good and faithful servant! You have been faithful with a few things; I will put you in charge of many things. Come and share your master's happiness!"
MATTHEW 25:21 NIV

Jesus told a parable about a master who gave three servants different amounts of money. Two of them invested, but the third buried his money. This parable has several applications, including investments in finances as well as gifts and talents. It's important that you use the gifts God gave you to make a difference in the world.

Are you investing in the lives of others with your talents?

DISRUPTIVE PERVERSION

Sexual immorality and all impurity or covetousness must not even be named among you, as is proper among saints.
EPHESIANS 5:3 ESV

Marriage is intended to display the beauty and mystery of God's redeeming work in reconciling the church to himself. The family reflects God's eternal inheritance fulfilled in the person of Christ. Sexual immorality is Satan's attempt to destroy, thwart, and diminish God's redemptive picture. Turn your thoughts to the Lord and flee from any mention of impurity.

Do you turn your face toward purity?

LOVE AND SACRIFICE

"Greater love has no one than this:
to lay down one's life for one's friends."
JOHN 15:13 NIV

Being strong may mean standing your ground and not letting your emotions get the best of you. Being a man of God involves love and sacrifice. The truest example of a man is in the person of Jesus. He deeply loved people. And in love, he made the ultimate sacrifice. Maybe you demonstrate love and sacrifice by setting aside your desires and putting someone else's needs first.

What does sacrifice look like to you?

CHRIST-CENTERED AIM

I press on toward the goal for the prize
of the upward call of God in Christ Jesus.

PHILIPPIANS 3:14 ESV

You must understand the underlying principles that drive you. Evaluate your motives and intentions to see what it is that fuels you. Without evaluation, you end up asking loved ones to fulfill what only Christ was meant to do. Fight valiantly to stay in the Word and keep yourself close to the person and the work of Jesus Christ.

Do you meditate on God's Word and search his precepts for truth?

THE HOLY SPIRIT

"When the Spirit of truth comes, he will guide you into all truth.
He will not speak on his own but will tell you what he has heard.
He will tell you about the future."
JOHN 16:13 NLT

There's a partner you can truly rely on—the Holy Spirit. As you deepen your relationship with God, ask him to fill you with the Holy Spirit. That partnership will give you a road map for your faith life. Consult your Counselor when you have questions and concerns. He will guide you when you are struggling.

In what areas do you need direction, guidance, or comfort?

ANXIETY STEALS

Do not be anxious about anything, but in everything by prayer and
supplication with thanksgiving let your request be made known to God.
PHILIPPIANS 4:6 ESV

The pressure of society can create such anxiety that it steals the beauty
around you. Your heart is best served by striving toward God's purpose while
embracing your current season. Don't look ahead if it causes you to neglect
what the Lord has blessed you with now. Whether you are in a season of
sorrow or joy, want or plenty, chaos or peace, make the best use of the time.

Do you trust your future to the Lord so you can live fully in the present?

FAITH OR DOUBT

"Put your finger here, and look at my hands.
Put your hand into the wound in my side.
Don't be faithless any longer. Believe!"
JOHN 20:27-28 NLT

Jesus didn't rebuke Thomas for doubting. He invited him to touch him and confirm his wounds. Faith and doubt may seem pitted against one another, but they actually complement each other. If you are having doubts about God, consider that it may strengthen your faith. It's okay to wrestle with God. Doubt is not a threat to your faith when you submit it to God.

Do you doubt God sometimes?

UNITING LOVE

Above all these put on love,
which binds everything together in perfect harmony.
COLOSSIANS 3:14 ESV

You may have a natural tendency to be over-disciplined if you are the type who strives for perfection. You might seek to maintain order by being too harsh with yourself and others. Or you may prefer an under-disciplined lifestyle as you fall into laziness or don't handle life's various responsibilities. The biblical stance has balance, produced by sacrificial love and grace.

Do you live in a way that brings harmony to your day?

COMPARISON

"If it is my will that he remain until I come, what is that to you?
You follow me!"
JOHN 21:22 ESV

When Jesus was talking to Peter about his life, Peter wanted to compare his future with another disciple's. Jesus basically said, "It's not your concern, Peter. You follow me." It seems the best cure for comparison is turning toward Jesus and following him. Think about any comparisons you might be making and turn to God instead.

What do you find yourself comparing most often?

DWELL IN THE WORD

Let the Word of Christ dwell in you richly, teaching and admonishing one another in all wisdom, singing psalms and hymns and spiritual songs, with thankfulness in your hearts to God.

COLOSSIANS 3:16 ESV

The true value of life permeates your humanity and is intrinsically linked to the spiritual life within you. Your life is not inherently yours; it's the breath of God blown into you. Saturate yourself with the breath of his Word and root yourself in the life source of God.

Are the words that flow from your mouth filled with thankfulness to God?

CHURCH COMMUNITY

They devoted themselves to the apostles' teaching and the fellowship,
to the breaking of bread and the prayers.
ACTS 2:42 ESV

The early followers of Jesus formed a community after his death, resurrection, and ascension. This was the first community church, but church has had different forms over the last two millennia. Community is essential for followers of Jesus. Are you plugged into a church community? The size and location don't matter; togetherness, breaking bread, and learning about God certainly do.

Do you have an active community of believers around you?

HOLINESS IN GOD

God has not called us for impurity, but in holiness.
1 THESSALONIANS 4:7 ESV

In an age of relativism, saturate your mind with a robust biblical view of the triune God. Do not settle for small glimpses of him but be filled with awe in the mighty pictures that Scripture paints of your Creator. Ground yourself in the knowledge that the confines of time are not able to restrain him. Only then can you have a proper respect for holiness.

Are you consumed by the need for holiness in God?

SHAME

There is now no condemnation for those who are in Christ Jesus,
because through Christ Jesus the law of the Spirit who gives life
has set you free from the law of sin and death.

ROMANS 8:1-2 NIV

As you find your worth and identity in Christ, you are encouraged not to
put any additional shame on yourself for the brokenness you have and will
experience. You should expect to make some mistakes because you are
broken, yet you are also redeemed. When you make mistakes, receive the
redemptive grace that Jesus provides.

What can you learn from your brokenness?

THANKFULNESS

We ought always to give thanks to God for you, brothers beloved by
the Lord, because God chose you as the first fruits to be saved, through
sanctification by the Spirit and belief in the truth.

2 THESSALONIANS 2:13 ESV

Gratitude postures your heart to see the gifts that have been given to you by
God. In turn, you'll live in a manner that brings him praise. There is a human
tendency to ruminate on what is missing from your life. Thankfulness focuses
on the one who blesses, who has given beyond all comprehension.

Are you stirred to thankfulness by your blessings?

TRUST

We know that God causes everything to work together for the good of those who love God and are called according to his purpose for them.
ROMANS 8:28 NLT

You can depend on the truth that when—not if—life gets hard, God is still present. If your health is poor, God is working. If your job is in jeopardy, God is working. If you can't get along with those around you, God is working. If you love God, you can trust him and know that he is still working.

Do you lean into God when things get bad?

SEARCH THE INTENTIONS

The aim of our charge is love that issues from a pure heart
and a good conscience and a sincere faith.
1 TIMOTHY 1:5 ESV

Be sensitive to the motives of your heart and keep watch on the intentions of your deeds. Your testimony depends on the integrity of your soul because it reflects outwardly through your character. You cannot hide who you truly are. Saturate yourself with the person of Christ, so his love is manifested in sacrificial deeds.

Are you drawn to your knees in the pursuit of a pure heart?

TRANSFORMATION

Do not conform to the pattern of this world, but be transformed by the renewing of your mind. Then you will be able to test and approve what God's will is—his good, pleasing and perfect will.
ROMANS 12:2 NIV

If you let it, culture will dominate your every thought and control your every action. Your deep spiritual transformation requires a movement of God not only in your heart but also in your mind. Renewal is needed within your thought life so you can ignore cultural distractions and fully focus on God.

What kind of mind shift needs to happen for you to see God more clearly?

MARATHON TRAINING

Rather train yourself for godliness.
1 TIMOTHY 4:7 ESV

"Rome wasn't built in a day." "Ball games are won in the off season." Sayings like this are marks in platforms that paint a picture of process. Spiritual, heart-based development takes a long time. Never take shortcuts on your path to sanctity. Don't despise the process. Buckle up for the long haul and embrace the fact that you are a work in progress.

Do you have the patience to endure your own personal development?

A STRONG FOUNDATION

"The rain came down, the streams rose, and the winds blew and beat against
that house; yet it did not fall, because it had its foundation on the rock."
MATTHEW 7:25 NIV

Storms in life can come out of nowhere and test you. Jesus told of a storm
that came from every direction, but the foundation of the house was solid, so
it stood the test. Your faith is built with engaged activity before the hard times
hit. Before you go through difficulties, you need consistent obedience to the
Word. That builds a strong foundation that can weather the storms.

Have you been building your strong foundation on the Word of God?

SUBMIT TO MENTORSHIP

Follow the pattern of the sound words that you have heard from me,
in faith and love that are in Christ Jesus.

2 TIMOTHY 1:13 ESV

Leadership is not for the faint of heart. To properly adhere to the biblical mandate of shining forth the character of Christ, you must be undergirded by the guidance of a biblically saturated mentor who engages openly with any shortcomings in you or himself. Seek solid men to surround you. Growth occurs around people who challenge you.

Do you have good and godly men around you?

FRUIT OF THE SPIRIT

The Holy Spirit produces this kind of fruit in our lives: love, joy, peace, patience, kindness, goodness, faithfulness, gentleness, and self-control.
GALATIANS 5:22-23 NLT

Relying on your own strength to be a man of God will cause you to fall short. Jesus embodied a righteous man, and God sent his Spirit to guide you and develop his righteous character. You require a good foundation in the Word and proper care in order to grow. You require the Holy Spirit as your guide. If you follow Jesus but you aren't exhibiting any of these qualities, ask God to fill you with his Holy Spirit.

Do you see the fruit of the Holy Spirit in your life?

GROW IN MATURITY

Flee youthful passions and pursue righteousness, faith, love, and peace, along with those who call on the Lord from a pure heart.

2 TIMOTHY 2:22 ESV

Biblical manhood is not saturated with shallow definitions of bench press markings, sexual mischievousness, or financial achievement. A godly man is defined by a Christlike attitude that is expressed in consistent sacrificial servitude for the good of others and the joy of God's heart.

Are you pouring out to others as well as being filled by the mercies of the gospel?

PROCESS

I am sure of this, that he who began a good work in you
will bring it to completion at the day of Jesus Christ.
PHILIPPIANS 1:6 ESV

It's hard to find any examples in the Bible of someone encountering God and immediately becoming a complete person. Even the apostle Paul said yes to God but still went through a long process to become the man God intended him to be. And after more years of ministry, Paul still confessed to areas where he fell short. Your life is a process. Don't feel rushed.

Are you aware of good growth in your relationship with God?

PURSUE HOLINESS

Strive for peace with everyone, and for the holiness
without which no one will see the Lord.
HEBREWS 12:14 ESV

Biblical truth does not convey independence amongst believers, but, rather,
a wholeness in the Christian community that is contingent upon each one
connecting to the Creator. Holiness is obtained through a divine union with
God though the work and person of Jesus Christ. Your distinction from the
world is your disposition. Pursue holiness.

Does your demeanor point directly to the Lord?

ATTITUDE

You must have the same attitude that Christ Jesus had.
PHILIPPIANS 2:5 NLT

From a very early age, people imitate the mannerisms, speech patterns, and facial expressions of those around them. As you grew up, you observed attitudes, behaviors, and demeanors; you did not only listen to words. Do you observe patterns in your behavior? The apostle Paul encourages us to have the same attitude as Jesus, which he later describes. Ultimately, he summed it up in one word: humility.

Does your attitude today reflect humility?

RELATIONSHIPS

As iron sharpens iron,
so a friend sharpens a friend.
PROVERBS 27:17 NLT

While you may prefer to be with people who are easygoing or always agree with you, it is in those seemingly more contentious relationships that your character is sharpened. As you parry with them back and forth, your arguments are honed, and your convictions are solidified. Those true friends give you many opportunities to practice patience, forgiveness, and grace, and you offer them the same.

Do you have iron in your life?

PARTNERSHIP

"It is not good for the man to be alone.
I will make a helper suitable for him."
GENESIS 2:18 NIV

God's intention was for his people to be in community. He even modeled that with the Trinity. Show your gratitude for your relationships and each of the roles they play in your life. Don't be afraid to have hard conversations about how you can support and encourage one another in Christ. You were never meant to do life alone, and God will show you that you don't have to.

Are you actively supporting a good friend through life?

IN HIS FOOTSTEPS

Whoever says he abides in him ought to walk
in the same way in which he walked.
1 JOHN 2:6 ESV

God created you to imitate his Son. Jesus came to show you what true humanity looks like. By his Spirit, and with his strength, you can emulate him. As you walk through today, ask the Spirit to align your heart with his ways for his glory.

Do you purposefully put your steps on the path where Jesus walked?

BRING PEACE

Let the peace of Christ rule in your hearts,
since as members of one body you were called to peace.
COLOSSIANS 3:15 NIV

The life of Christ attested to mercy, humility, love, and sacrifice, not a dominating force. The only way to have true peace is by way of Christ. When there is chaos in your life, try on a godly demeanor before engaging in the situation. It may feel counterintuitive, but you'll be modeling the way of Jesus by doing so.

Are you able to adopt the peace of Christ amidst the chaos in your life?

TRANSPARENCY

If we confess our sins, he is faithful and just to forgive us our sins
and to cleanse us from all unrighteousness.
1 JOHN 1:9 ESV

Strength is not an innate or self-generated characteristic; rather, it is grounded
in a deep dependency on the Lord. Confessing your sin causes you to gravitate
toward the God who sustains, restores, and redeems. As a man, it is imperative
to demonstrate the humility of confession, first to the Lord and then to your
accountability partners. Not only does it demonstrate the supremacy of Christ
in your life, but it also models a clear picture of gospel living.

Do you humbly and transparently confess your sin to God and others?

TO THE MOUNTAIN

The eleven disciples went to Galilee, to the mountain where Jesus had told
them to go. When they saw him, they worshiped him; but some doubted.

MATTHEW 28:16-17 NIV

When the disciples got to the mountain and saw Jesus, some worshiped
and others *doubted*. That word means to "stand in two places." All of them
were there physically, but some were spiritually or emotionally elsewhere.
Jesus didn't make their reality in that moment a prerequisite for his Great
Commission. In the next verse, he gave this group instructions to go and
change the world. Clearly, Jesus welcomes those who are struggling.

If you doubt, are you willing to keep moving ahead for Jesus' sake?

LOVE THE CHURCH

By this we know that we love the children of God,
when we love God and obey his commandments.
1 JOHN 5:2 ESV

It's important that you model an affinity for the saints, but it's only sustainable through a relationship with the Holy Spirit. Engagement with local believers allows you to see God's will in the life of the church. Service to the children of God aligns you with God's redemptive work which brings restoration to you and to others.

How do you get along with other believers?

ANGER

Human anger does not produce the righteousness God desires.
JAMES 1:20 NLT

Anger is not the issue; how you manage anger is what's imperative. Consider your anger and how it affects you and the people you love. Are you able to express it in love, or do you simply hurt people with your words and behavior? Anger affects relationships. Seek the righteousness God desires when you feel yourself getting angry.

Does your anger change the way you feel about the person you are angry with?

SUPREMACY OF CHRIST

Since therefore the children share in flesh and blood, he himself likewise partook of the same things, that through death he might destroy the one who has the power of death that is, the devil.
HEBREWS 2:14 ESV

Children can detect inconsistencies in their parents and also find disparities in themselves. It is essential that you live transparently with your sin. Though the sinfulness of your heart can be heinous, the magnitude of the cross conveys the message that the love of Christ stretches as far as the east is from the west. Point your life toward the cross of Christ.

Do you allow the supremacy of Christ to shine brightly on your sins?

ACTION

Don't just listen to God's word. You must do what it says.
Otherwise, you are only fooling yourselves.
JAMES 1:22 NLT

Following Jesus means standing with the marginalized, the poor, and the broken because faith without works is dead. How can you model this behavior? How do you interact with people of different ethnicities, economic, or educational levels? Be bold in your behavior and stand for justice.

Are you actively seeking ways to defend those who can't stand up for themselves?

RESPECT

Hear, my son, your father's instruction,
and forsake not your mother's teaching.
PROVERBS 1:8 ESV

Respect for authority is a learned trait. You can acquire it by observing a father who lives respectfully. No earthly father is perfect, but if his heart is submitted to God, he will instill a posture of respect that will permeate into his entire family. Take some time today to reflect upon the father that God gave to you.

What instruction did your father provide that you carry with you to this day?

LOVE DEEPLY

Above all, love each other deeply,
because love covers over a multitude of sins.
1 PETER 4:8 NIV

Loving someone deeply means you will be less prone to the effects and the brokenness of sin. Sin is still real and present, but love is more powerful. Deeply felt love has the power to cover and heal sin. You are going to make mistakes, but if you continuously move toward love, you will experience spiritual coverage as you are healed and restored.

Are you prepared to love so deeply that even sin is affected by that love?

GRATEFUL HEARTS

Children are a heritage from the LORD,
the fruit of the womb a reward.
PSALM 127:3 ESV

Scripture tells us that children embody the miracle of life. They bear God's beauty and majesty. Reflect on the children God has brought into your life, whether they are yours, the neighbor's, or the kids that scamper underfoot in the church lobby. God has granted you the opportunity to show them that their lives hold value. Shower them with the love that flows from the Father.

Are you treating the children in your life with God's intentional love?

HOSPITALITY

Cheerfully share your home with those who
need a meal or a place to stay.
1 PETER 4:9 NLT

Being intentional and cheerful with visitors is important no matter what your
home is like, how great the meal is, or how long they stay. There is something
sacred about sharing a meal together. When you break bread and talk about
life and faith, it's a holy moment. In Revelation, Jesus speaks of knocking at a
door and sharing a meal. Perhaps there's something to that.

Do you open your home to guests?

STOREHOUSE OF WEALTH

I have stored up your word in my heart,
that I might not sin against you.
PSALM 119:11 ESV

How amazing would it be to have your friends and family as the recipients of the treasures in God's Word. Be intentional about keeping the Scriptures central in your life. Model sobriety when handling the text. Saturate the minds of your loved ones, remembering that Jesus said, "Apart from me you can do nothing" (John 15:5).

Do you store God's Word in your heart as an amazing stronghold against sin?

HUMILITY OR TRUST

If you bow low in God's awesome presence,
he will eventually exalt you as you leave the timing in his hands.
1 PETER 5:6 TPT

Usually, climbing to the top of the corporate ladder conflicts with humility and trust; those traits are seen as weak or passive. Believers, however, must humble themselves. Showing weakness may cause others to distrust you, but you follow a God who, in Jesus, submitted himself to death on a cross because of his humility. Trust that your humility will lead to greater things.

Do you trust God to cover your humility with his strength?

TRUE IDENTITY

"Truly, truly, I say to you, the Son can do nothing of his own accord, but only what he sees the Father doing. For whatever the Father does, that the Son does likewise."

JOHN 5:19 ESV

Jesus found his identity in the Father. Most sons grasp their worth through the love of their earthly father or lack thereof. As you look to Christ, let the river of life flow from him into you. This establishes your foundation for a Christ-centered identity that is firmly rooted in biblical truth. Identity is grounded in the Creator, not the creation.

How can you fix your eyes on your heavenly Father for your true identity?

NO ROOM

Do not love this world nor the things it offers you, for when you love the world, you do not have the love of the Father in you.

1 JOHN 2:15 NLT

You probably know what leads you in the wrong direction. Consider what is it like to be so filled with God's love that you wouldn't have room for the things of this world? The goal is not to escape but to be immune to the world because your heart is already full of the wonder of God.

What can you do today to increase God's love in your heart?

CHARACTER

I therefore, a prisoner for the Lord, urge you to walk in a manner worthy of the calling to which you have been called.

EPHESIANS 4:1 ESV

Walking with integrity is the hallmark of the Christian faith. Your call to salvation is intended to exemplify God's character, quality, and virtue. The Father's decree, then, is to lead his children to be unique image bearers who reflect his grandeur, wonder, and glory. When you model good character, you also teach Christian virtue.

Do you sometimes wonder what unbelievers see in you as a follower of God?

PAIN AND JOY

"He will wipe every tear from their eyes, and there will be no more death or sorrow or crying or pain. All these things are gone forever."
REVELATION 21:4 NLT

The hope you have in Jesus leads to an eternal life with no sadness. Is it possible to live now with that hope in your soul? At a young age, kids understand both joy and pain. Growing older tends to complicate things. Image a world with no more pain, suffering, or sadness. Imagine pure joy all the time. This is what hope in Jesus looks like—permanent joy!

Does your hope extend to your eternal reality with pure joy?

TEACH WITH TRAJECTORY

Set your minds on things that are above,
not on things that are on earth.
COLOSSIANS 3:2 ESV

In defiance of instant gratification, it's good to view life as a trajectory. Your choices today impact the pathways into tomorrow. Your life is not merely what your eyes now see but also what the Lord has promised later. The love, compassion, sacrifice, and service forged now for the sake of the gospel will have a ripple effect into eternity.

Is your eternal impact something you keep at the forefront of your mind?

NEWNESS

"Look, I am making everything new!" And then he said to me,
"Write this down, for what I tell you is trustworthy and true."
REVELATION 21:5 NLT

Each day is a new opportunity to grow your faith, to show someone God's love, or to breathe deeply of his presence. God promised to make us new. Everything will be made new. Where do you need renewing? Consider the newness of each day; it's another opportunity to love the people in your life.

What do you need to be reminded about in order to revisit God's newness?

OVERCOMING PROCRASTINATION

If a man is lazy, the rafters sag;
if his hands are idle, the house leaks.
ECCLESIASTES 10:18 NIV

You may clear your dishes as soon as you're done eating and put them directly into the dishwasher, or you might leave them lying around and only wash them when you need a plate. One is a disciplined behavior, and one reeks of procrastination. Both are learned. If you've learned to be a fantastic procrastinator, you can also learn to be a wonderfully disciplined man.

Do you tend toward a more disciplined or lazy lifestyle?

SMALL BEGINNINGS

"Do not despise these small beginnings,
for the LORD rejoices to see the work begin."
ZECHARIAH 4:10 NLT

Each big achievement began with the smallest step, like the rebuilding of the Lord's temple. Before the interior was the roof. Before the roof, the walls. Before the walls was the floor. Before the floor was the foundation. And the foundation began with a single brick—a crucial, small beginning. You may have grand goals for yourself, but you can't achieve them without a small beginning.

Have you been delaying that first, small step in a grand vision?

DEPENDENCE ON CHRIST

God chose what is foolish in the world to shame the wise;
God chose what is weak in the world to shame the strong.
1 CORINTHIANS 1:27 ESV

People don't need a superman who can fix all the unsolvable problems of the world; they need a committed, God-honoring man who lives his life on his knees in total submission to the Lord. They need to see the air you breathe, the bread you eat, the God who leads you, and the obedience that comes by faith. Your intentional, dependent life and reliance on God are complementary to faithful living.

Does dependence on Christ give you peace?

FAVORITES

Now Israel [Jacob] loved Joseph more than all of his children.
GENESIS 37:3 NKJV

Playing favorites was nothing new to Jacob's family. His mother preferred him over his brother. When Jacob favored Joseph, he set Joseph up for big problems with his brothers. Each person has different gifts. You may be tempted to consider some of God's gifts greater than others or favoring certain people. This can create resentment. Pay attention to the way you show your love to family and friends.

Do you find yourself respecting some of God's gifts over others?

HOPE

Hope deferred makes the heart sick,
but a dream fulfilled is a tree of life.
PROVERBS 13:12 NLT

Don't put off hope. You could potentially delay the pursuit of your best desires under the guise of staying safe or being prudent. But God invites you into his adventure. True peace comes from seizing the invitation to live a God-centered life. It almost always requires risk, but the reward is the rich and satisfying life you were created to live. Don't delay your blessing; step into your dream today.

Do you hear God's voice in the dreams that stir your heart?

LISTEN

"Hear O Israel: the LORD our God, the LORD is one."
DEUTERONOMY 6:4 NIV

God's people must listen as God is described for who he truly is. You are surrounded by gods that "are not gods" (Jeremiah 16:20). You must call others to acknowledge the Lord so they will not be confused. You need to speak honestly, clearly, and consistently about who God is, and you can only do this when you know him personally.

Are you ready to listen to the one true God, knowing who he really is?

CHOSEN

You are a chosen race, a royal priesthood, a holy nation, a people for his possession, so that you may proclaim the praises of the one who called you out of darkness into his marvelous light.

1 PETER 2:9 CSB

God intentionally picked you. He didn't settle for you, and he didn't begrudgingly accept you; he chose you on purpose and for a purpose. You have been called into a role of great significance: you're an ambassador for Jesus Christ. You have an endless supply of spiritual VIP passes to hand out. Let others know how important they are to God.

How grateful are you to be chosen by God?

TOTAL LOVE

"Love the LORD your God with all your heart
and with all your soul and with all your strength."
DEUTERONOMY 6:5 NIV

Once you have acknowledged the "who" of God, a response is required. The right response is to love God with all that you are. This love is full and complete—all of your heart, your soul, and your strength. You have a daily opportunity to not only love the Lord totally but to show this same love to others.

Do you demonstrate an active love for God in your daily life?

SPEAKING LIFE

"Don't be afraid," he said, "for you are very precious to God. Peace!
Be encouraged! Be strong!" As he spoke these words to me,
I suddenly felt stronger.

DANIEL 10:19 NLT

God's Word has the power to invigorate you. When you actively search for
what he is saying, you will find a vitality and strength you might otherwise
miss. You can also speak those words to others to bring them life. God has
gifted you with the wonderful power of his words, and he encourages you to
share them freely.

Do you feel God's strength flowing into you when you hear his Word?

COMMIT

"You must commit yourselves wholeheartedly to these commands
that I am giving you today."
DEUTERONOMY 6:6 NLT

The way you obey God's commands reveals much about your commitment
to him. Being committed means more than just knowing the commands;
you need to follow them and understand that they keep you focused on him.
They also protect you. When you show your total commitment to God's
commands, those around you see where your heart is.

Are you ready to wholeheartedly know and obey God's commands?

GROWING GOOD

Let us not become weary in doing good,
for at the proper time we will reap a harvest if we do not give up.
GALATIANS 6:9 NIV

When you do good, you might wonder if it's worth it. People don't seem to notice, and life can be full of troubles. Don't give up. Each time you do good, a seed is planted, and a life centered on Jesus creates an environment for those seeds to grow. You may not know the result of every good deed, but you can trust that God does, and he is growing them to their fullest potential.

Do you find it difficult to keep doing good when you don't see results?

REPEAT

"Repeat them again and again to your children. Talk about them when you are at home and when you are on the road, when you are going to bed and when you are getting up."
DEUTERONOMY 6:7 NLT

Learning happens best with repetition. The commands of God are not just a way to live but an important step in order to know and understand the ways of Jesus. You will learn them by reading, thinking, and talking about them. When you become absorbed in the Word, studying it on repeat, it overflows in your speech, behavior, and motivation.

Do you ponder God's Word throughout your day?

WISDOM

With God are wisdom and might;
he has counsel and understanding.
JOB 12:13 ESV

When the Creator made the universe, he knew you would be naturally drawn to him through his work and creativity. God and wisdom are one and the same. When you are closely aligned with your heavenly Father, you are more likely to know which decisions to make. The act of decision-making becomes an act of worship as you rely on your relationship with God to lead the way.

Are you drawn into God's presence when you have a decision to make?

TIE THEM ON

"Tie them to your hands and wear them on your foreheads as reminders."
DEUTERONOMY 6:8 NLT

When you tie God's commandments to your hands, you're acting on them.
Wearing the commandments on your forehead means you're transparent
about the God you serve. You talk about Jesus and are unafraid to share
your motivation for your actions. These things are not busy work. They're
incredibly important and valuable as a demonstration of your faith.

Do you love the Lord's commandments?

PEACE AND STRENGTH

The LORD gives his people strength.
The LORD blesses them with peace.
PSALM 29:11 NLT

God gives you strength and blesses you with peace. When you go through challenges, you may be tempted to dig deep to find the strength to carry on. Instead, you should reach out to God as the source of true strength. God has an endless supply, and he wants to bless you with his strength and his peace.

Do you recognize when you are attempting to draw from your own strength?

WRITE THEM DOWN

"Write them on the doorposts of your house and on your gates."
DEUTERONOMY 6:9 NLT

Are you a walking advertisement for a clothing name brand? Perhaps you simply like the style or the fit, but usually the brand means something. When you write God's commandments on your doorposts, you're advertising him. Your acceptance of Christ means you put him on display; he is your brand, and you belong to him. There's no catchy phrase, only love, mercy, and grace.

Do you clothe yourself in God's commandments?

WORKING IN YOU

God is working in you, giving you the desire and the power
to do what pleases him.

PHILIPPIANS 2:13 ESV

God does not give you a list of demands as he is calling you to work for the kingdom. He doesn't leave you to sort out what he wants you to accomplish. He uses his power to strengthen you. He is both the motivation and the destination for your spiritual life. When you draw close to him, he begins to produce in you the desire to do whatever pleases him.

Do you think about different ways to please God?

BE STRONG

"Be strong and courageous, for you must go with this people into the land
that the LORD swore to their ancestors to give them."
DEUTERONOMY 31:7 NIV

God didn't simply give his people a set of rules; he entered the world and
the lives of his people through his Son. He was tempted, hungry, and thirsty.
He slept, worked, and laughed. He confronted sin. He engaged in the world
around him. This required strength and courage. A good leader, like Christ,
lives alongside those he leads.

Do you try to demonstrate Christ-like strength and courage to those you lead?

STRONGHOLD

The LORD is good,
a stronghold in a day of distress;
he cares for those who take refuge in him.
NAHUM 1:7 CSB

God is good, and he promises to give you safety in times of trouble. You must, however, be willing to go to him. He does this so that you will always keep in mind that he is the true source of your protection. In the act of retreating to God, you make great advances against your enemy and deal an incredible blow to anything intended to harm you.

How can anything harm you if it is the exact thing that brings you closer to God?

WONDERFULLY MADE

I praise you because I am fearfully
and wonderfully made:
Your works are wonderful,
I know that full well.
PSALM 139:14 NIV

People expect a lot from each other. Community involves significant time and effort as you support your friends and family through life's various challenges and events. And, once in a while, you need help from them. Even in those moments, God's truth rings out: humans are fearfully and wonderfully made.

Do you see your time helping friends and family as a blessing?

COMPLETELY NEW

If anyone is in Christ, he is a new creation;
the old has passed away, and see, the new has come!
2 CORINTHIANS 5:17 CSB

The promise of following Jesus is for a new life! The transforming power of God is so strong that it erases your old desires and ways of thinking. When you forget this, you carry the weight of your mistakes around and slow your own growth. You are a new creation, having been made new simply by choosing to follow Jesus. You don't need to worry about your past any longer. Keep living in the direction of Jesus.

Are your eyes open to the ways God is renewing you?

GENTLENESS

A soft answer turns away wrath,
but a harsh word stirs up anger.
PROVERBS 15:1 NIV

A display of gentleness is evidence of the Holy Spirit dwelling in your heart. The way you speak to people reveals the degree to which God's Word influences you. There's always that one person who requires an extra measure of grace; the way you respond is directly proportional to the grace you have received. God gives grace freely, so you should do the same.

Can you acknowledge the Holy Spirit working in you as you speak gentle words?

WHAT'S INSIDE

"Do not look on his appearance or on the height of his stature,
because I have rejected him. For the LORD sees not as man sees:
man looks on the outward appearance, but the LORD looks on the heart."
1 SAMUEL 16:7 ESV

God often chooses unexpected people to accomplish his goals. The only
person you're likely to assess accurately is yourself, and even then, you will
probably flatten God's criteria. God is able to look at the heart, and he often
uncovers positive traits even you have overlooked. He draws out of you
deeper strength than you knew you possessed.

Do you go to God to find out more about you?

MAINTAIN JUSTICE

Return to your God;
maintain love and justice,
and wait for your God always.
MICAH 6:8 NKJV

Jesus was the physical representation of justice. He healed. He cast out demons. He brought hope. He righted wrongs. And he paid the penalty for your sins in an ultimate act of justice. You act justly when you behave as he did. God's justice is not only final; it is also complete. And it is hopeful. As you act justly with those around you, may you also be filled with hope.

How can you maintain justice in difficult situations?

STRONGER TOGETHER

If either of them falls down, one can help the other up.
But pity anyone who falls and has no one to help them up.
ECCLESIASTES 4:10 NIV

Our culture celebrates the stoic man who faces his battles singlehandedly. The lone wolf is seen as the ultimate in masculine strength. Ironically, such a man is likely the most vulnerable. Only weak people believe that receiving help is a sign of weakness. In the same way that you delight in offering strength to others, there are others who are eager to offer their strength to you. Your strength can be multiplied by those you are with.

Are you a lone wolf or are you willing to seek strength through others?

LOVE MERCY

The LORD has told you what is good,
and this is what he requires of you:
to do what is right, to love mercy,
and to walk humbly with your God.
MICAH 6:8 NLT

Mercy is what God gives you; without it, you are hopeless and lost. You love receiving mercy from God because you know you're caught in the twisted mess of life. Consider giving mercy to others when punishment is deserved. This is God's heart.

Do you love to give mercy to those who need it?

KNOW YOUR FLOCK

Be sure you know the condition of your flocks,
give careful attention to your herds.
PROVERBS 27:23 NIV

It's not enough to simply watch for trouble in the lives of your friends and family. You can easily lose the pulse of a normal rhythm in your everyday relationships, but you must give special care to your own flock. When trouble comes, you'll then be prepared for it. In fact, you're likely to catch trouble earlier if you already know the condition of another's spiritual life.

Do you carefully watch over the lives of your friends and family?

WALKING HUMBLY

He guides the humble in what is right
and teaches them his way.
PSALM 25:9 NIV

Taking walks is good for the body and the soul. Being intentional about inviting others to join requires humility. One will walk faster. One may want to pause to look at something. One might want to walk further. Humility will be required to walk peaceably. Walking with God is no different. His ways are not your ways. Where he goes, you follow. Walk in humility and bring others along. This journey is not supposed to be a solo experience.

Are you humble when you walk with others?

REST

It is useless for you to work so hard from early morning until late at night,
anxiously working for food to eat;
for God gives rest to his loved ones.

PSALM 127:2 NLT

Failure to rest is usually a failure to trust God. There are many valid things you could do with your time. The danger comes when you forget that rest is one of them. God disapproves of laziness, but it's also sinful to not rest. Work will never supply the rest that God offers. With rest, you will remember your dependence on him.

Do you take regular times to rest?

SELF-SACRIFICE

"The Kingdom of Heaven is like a treasure that a man discovered hidden in a field. In his excitement, he hid it again and sold everything he owned to get enough money to buy the field."
MATTHEW 13:44 NLT

You sacrifice a lot for the things you most desire. There is a cost for the big house, the nice car, and even your new job. But there is something greater and more worthy of sacrifice—God's kingdom. Jesus tells us that God's kingdom is so valuable that it would be like finding a treasure hidden in a field, then selling everything you own to buy it.

What might it look like for you to pursue God's kingdom with such intensity?

EVERYTHING YOU DO

Let everything you do reflect the integrity
and seriousness of your teaching.
TITUS 2:7 NLT

The only way to demonstrate that you really mean what you say is to live it.
Your actions are your primary way of teaching; your own life is the ultimate
visual aid for anything you want to convey. The best way to instruct is the
one-two punch of teaching and modeling. You must live correctly and speak
about why you have chosen to live that way. People around you will learn
from your life whatever it teaches.

Are you living with a one-two punch?

MOST IMPORTANT LESSON

"This is how God loved the world: He gave his one and only son, so that everyone who believes in him will not perish but have eternal life."
JOHN 3:16 NLT

This text is important because in it you find the entirety of gospel message. Of all the things you learn in life, this is the most important. A great way to comprehend the impact of this Scripture is to read the verse, replacing "the world" and "everyone" with your name and then with the names of those around you. Do this often, and you will understand the greatest message.

Have you grasped the impact of God's choice to have his Son pay for your sins?

TELL THEM

Parents will tell their children what you have done.
They will retell your mighty acts.
PSALM 145:4 NCV

Throughout your life, God has worked to transform, bless, and bring you wisdom. You're the expert in what he has done. It's effective to relay messages through stories. You can share the ways God has worked in your life as a powerful testimony. Explain how God has changed you. The God of the Bible is at work in you right now.

Do you realize the power of your testimony and your stories about the Lord's impact in your life?

GIVING GOOD GIFTS

"If you sinful people know how to give good gifts to your children, how much more will your Father in Heaven give the Holy Spirit to those who ask?"
LUKE 11:13 NLT

Most fathers enjoy giving gifts to their children. Giving a child what they want indicates that a father has clearly heard the request. Your Father in heaven also knows what is in your best interests. The Holy Spirit is God's gift to you. As you think of the gifts you received as a child, remember that they are symbolic of the gifts the Father has for you now.

Do you recognize God's gifts for you?

WARNING AND PATIENCE

We urge you, brothers and sisters, warn those who are idle and disruptive,
encourage the disheartened, help the weak, be patient with everyone.
1 THESSALONIANS 5:14 NIV

Correction without patience easily becomes anger. Patience without
correction results in avoidance. Being a godly leader requires both, but
properly balanced. The Bible urges you to follow God's example when you are
encouraging right living in others. The process falls apart if not done properly
with encouragement, strength, and patience. Those are the three main
ingredients of godly direction.

Are you able to strike the right balance between patience and boldness?

DON'T SHRINK

"I never shrank back from telling you what you needed to hear,
either publicly or in your homes."
ACTS 20:20 NLT

Confrontation is difficult, but it's necessary. Paul did not shrink back from
telling people what they needed to hear. You must not be afraid to speak the
truth either. You must confront people about their sins in order for them to
hear the gospel and the good news of Jesus Christ.

Do you have the courage to confront rather than to shrink back?

SAFETY IN NUMBERS

Where there is no guidance, a people falls,
but in an abundance of counselors there is safety.
PROVERBS 11:14 ESV

Fathers have incredible physical, emotional, and—especially—spiritual responsibility in raising children. But within the body of the church, you can find wisdom and support. There are times when you simply don't have the answers you need for the children you are investing in. Christians have community for God's glory and his purposes.

Do you know when to seek wisdom and counseling from God's people?

HONORING PARENTS

Children, obey your parents because you belong to the Lord,
for this is the right thing to do. "Honor your father and mother."
EPHESIANS 6:1-2 NLT

Honor is determined by attitude. As an adult, you no longer need to obey your parents, but you are supposed to honor them. You show honor when you ask for advice, speak kindly, take care of something they need, or defer to an activity they choose. It's Biblical to honor your parents by acknowledging their wisdom and their sacrifices.

How can you show respect and defer to your parents today?

CALLED UP

"You should select from all the people able men, God-fearing, trustworthy, and hating dishonest profit. Place them over the people as commanders of thousands, hundreds, fifties, and tens."

EXODUS 18:21 CSB

God recruits men with hearts pointed toward him. He is less concerned about skill and experience, and more concerned about motivation and love. Men who are intentionally living for Jesus are the most likely to be called into faithful action. If you wait to be called before you begin conditioning, you will be woefully underprepared.

Do you have a daily practice of seeking the Lord?

HOPE

"The same thing is true of the words I speak.
They will not return to me empty."
ISAIAH 55:11 NCV

As a Christian, you should look for ways to teach and train others in the faith. Offer to take people to church, join small groups, share meals, and pray for people. Sometimes those same people make decisions that lead them away from Jesus. You might feel crushed or frustrated. But Isaiah 55:11 is filled with hope. The faithfulness of God's Word is always fruitful. It will not return empty.

Do you feel deflated when the work you have poured into others seems to be for nothing?

YOUNG EXAMPLES

Let no one despise you for your youth, but set the believers an example in speech, in conduct, in love, in faith, in purity.
1 TIMOTHY 4:12 ESV

While God is using you to teach others, he is also revealing himself to you through them. Some traits of God are best demonstrated through youthful innocence and purity. If you pay close attention, you'll see the nature of God in younger Christians. When you do, celebrate it, and encourage them. Let them know that God is using them right now, in their youth, to teach others about himself.

Do you see the work of the Lord in the younger believers in your life?

COURAGE

Be watchful, stand firm in the faith, act like men, be strong.
Let all that you do be done in love.
1 CORINTHIANS 16:13-14 ESV

A godly man is alert, stands firm in the faith, is strong, and does everything in love. He is aware of what's going on in people's lives. He passes along his faith through words and actions and doesn't give up when conflicts arise. None of this is possible without Christ dwelling in him. It takes courage to be a godly man, but you can do it with his strength.

How do you stand firm in your faith?

FULLNESS

To know Christ's love that surpasses knowledge,
so that you may be filled with all the fullness of God.
EPHESIANS 3:19 CSB

Christ's love brings fullness into your life. He sacrificed his life on your
behalf. It is through that amazing love that you are invited into a rich and
satisfying life. The promise of his love makes you complete. Your life is
transformed, and you are able to live with more power and purpose than you
ever could alone. Through that power you can help others experience the
same amazing love and fullness of life.

Are you filled with the fullness of God?

ENCOURAGE

Fathers, do not provoke your children, lest they become discouraged.
COLOSSIANS 3:21 NKJV

Paul told the Colossians to put off things that lead to spiritual death and provoke: anger, wrath, malice, blasphemy, and lying. Once those are off, you put on tender mercies, kindness, humility, meekness, long-suffering, bearing with one another, forgiveness, and love. You are ruled by the peace of God and allow Christ's words to live in you. When you do not provoke others, it encourages them. They trust you, and in turn they demonstrate these new qualities to others.

How can you stop yourself from provoking people?

WHO TO IMITATE

I urge you to imitate me.
1 CORINTHIANS 4:16 CSB

You're a Christian not just because someone told you about Jesus, but because they also demonstrated what it means to live a Christ-centered life. For every Christian, there is a line of imitators who each connect back to Jesus himself. Your job is to live in such a way that you also are an imitator of the Lord. Your imitation of him becomes an invitation to those around you.

Is an invitation to live like you also an invitation to live like Jesus?

EAT MEAT

Solid food is for those who are mature, who through training who have the skill to recognize the difference between right and wrong.

HEBREWS 5:14 NLT

As you grow older, your eating habits change, and you adjust. What made you feel full as a baby barely made a dent when you were child, and it does nothing for you as an adult. The same is true for spiritual nourishment. When you were young, you received spiritual milk. As you got older, you dug into meatier concepts like sin, salvation, and the Trinity. Continue to look for ways to be spiritually mature.

Are you still drinking from a bottle, or do you have your steak knife ready?

WORSHIP THE SPLENDOR

Honor the LORD for the glory of his name.
Worship the LORD in the splendor of his holiness.
PSALM 29:2 NLT

Worshiping God is the only natural response to his power. Intimacy with God results in worship, and worship comes as a result of focusing on God's power and goodness. In times of difficulty, rely on his strength to protect you. In times of joy, celebrate his power working within you. In all situations you benefit by placing your focus on the splendor of God.

Do you love to worship the Lord just because of the glory of his name?

THE CLOSEST FISH

"Follow me, and I will make you fishers of men."
MATTHEW 4:19 NKJV

At the end of his ministry, Jesus told his followers to go out and make disciples, beginning nearby in Jerusalem and spreading to the ends of the earth. You have fish nearby as well—the people you interact with every day. You have all the equipment necessary, and because you are in relationship with them, you have a great opportunity to share the gospel.

How can you be a fisher of men?

COMFORT

Even when I go through the darkest valley,
I fear no danger, for you are with me;
your rod and your staff—they comfort me.
PSALM 23:4 CSB

You may focus on the gentle, comforting God, and forget that one of the primary roles of your Shepherd is to be your defender. It is in the dark, terrifying places that you are aware of your true source of safety. Perhaps this is the reason God leads you through the dark seasons. Your heavenly Father protects you with his might, and that should bring you deep peace.

Do you remember to go to your Father when you need a safe harbor?

DISCIPLINE WITH LOVE

"The Lord disciplines those he loves,
and he punishes each one he accepts as his child."
HEBREWS 12:6 NLT

Loving discipline has one goal: restoration. It seeks to connect people, to right wrongs, and to demonstrate justice and peace. The greatest example of God's discipline is his love. He disciplines you through the consequences of your choices. He convicts you through Scripture and the Holy Spirit. He allows consequences because his desire is for you to be restored to him. You are not only loved by him; you belong to him.

Do you see God's love in your consequences?

WEARY

Even youths shall faint and be weary,
and young men shall fall exhausted;
but they who wait for the LORD shall renew their strength.
ISAIAH 40:30 ESV

When you trust that God is at work and you're simply assisting him, you'll find a deep supply of energy to keep doing his will. The next time you're exhausted, pause and talk to God. He may encourage you to keep going, he may insist that you stop to rest, or he may convict you to shed some sin. No matter how he responds, he promises to help you.

How's your energy level today?

DIVINE DISCIPLINE

As you endure this divine discipline, remember that God is treating you as his own children. Who ever heard of a child not disciplined by its father?
HEBREWS 12:7 NLT

The question is rhetorical. When God disciplines you, he is demonstrating that you are his. The fact that you endure it is evidence of being in the hands of a loving Father. A father must discipline his child. If a child is not disciplined, they really don't belong to anyone.

How have you experienced the discipline of God?

CONSTANT CONNECTION

"I am the vine; you are the branches. The one who remains in me and I in him produces much fruit, because you can do nothing without me."

JOHN 15:5 CSB

You may be tempted to treat God like a turbo boost when things become hard. If today's verse were written as a reflection of how most live, it would say, "Apart from me you can do most things." But Jesus knew exactly what he was saying. Don't only rely on him as some sort of power-up in the bad times. You are designed for constant connection.

Do you have a constant connection to Christ?

STAY ALERT

Be sober, be vigilant; because your adversary the devil walks about
like a roaring lion, seeking whom he may devour.
1 PETER 5:8 NKJV

Being sober means having a clear mind and to be alert. When you are
vigilant, you look both inwardly and outwardly, preparing to face the
adversary. Soberness and vigilance will prepare you for his arrival. God's
Word familiarizes you with the roar of the lion, so you know what to do
when he appears.

How do you prepare yourself for the attack of the lion?

ACCURATE PICTURE

Fathers, do not make your children angry,
but raise them with the training and teaching of the Lord.
EPHESIANS 6:4 NCV

Is your first understanding of God connected to how you experienced your earthly father? Fathers are models of the Lord whether they intend to be or not. A child with a strict father can assume that God is judgmental. An absent father may leave a perception of God as uncaring. As you release anger and walk in forgiveness, you get a more accurate picture of God and your own father.

How did your earthly father teach you about your heavenly Father?

ONE GENERATION

When all that generation had been gathered to their fathers,
another generation arose after them who did not know the LORD
nor the work which He had done for Israel.

JUDGES 2:10 NKJV

God instructed Moses about worship, the tabernacle, and other things.
Despite being told to remember, they forgot in one generation. They still
followed the rituals, but they didn't know why. It's your role as a Christian to
talk about the amazing things God has done. Praise him for his work in you,
and let the next generation hear so they remember.

Are you bold about what God has done in your life?

BIGGER

I pray that you, being rooted and established in love, may have power, together with all the Lord's holy people, to grasp how wide and long and high and deep is the love of Christ.

EPHESIANS 3:17-18 NIV

Full understanding of God begins when his power becomes reality. As your understanding grows, you realize that he exceeds your ability to understand. Some people refuse to chase the Holy Spirit into the unknown which stunts spiritual growth. He wants you to experience a deeper satisfaction in your relationship with him.

Do you allow the Holy Spirit to take you into uncomfortable spaces for the sake of your spiritual growth?

WASHING FEET

Then he began to wash the disciples' feet,
drying them with the towel he had around him.
JOHN 13:5 NLT

There are people in your life who you are called to love, and one of the easiest ways is to serve them. Each day you can wash the feet of those around you through selfless, sometimes humiliating, acts of service. You can show mercy and grace when judgment is warranted. You can spend time with them in ways that honor them and not you. Serve like Jesus.

As you serve Jesus, are you serving the people around you?

INFINITELY MORE

All glory to God, who is able, through his mighty power at work within us,
to accomplish infinitely more than we might ask or think.
EPHESIANS 3:20 NLT

The Father takes joy in doing things for you that exceed your expectations.
He wants you to stare at him in wonder and come to the realization he
is much more impressive than you give him credit for. You might think
that you aren't worth his time, but he wants your life to be abundant. The
power of God is most beautifully demonstrated in his ability to exceed your
expectations.

Do you open yourself up to the abundance of life that God wants for you?

DISCERNMENT

"You must distinguish between the unclean and the clean."
LEVITICUS 11:47 NIV

Throughout the Bible, people struggled to discern between evil and good. Cain brought God an unrighteous offering. David pursued Bathsheba. Solomon was led astray. Peter refused to eat with Gentile believers. Your mind can discern between wrong and right by the work of the Holy Spirit. When you pray for wisdom, also ask for the desire to do the right thing.

Are you using the wisdom of the Holy Spirit to discern between evil and good?

SEARCH THE SCRIPTURES

"You search the Scriptures because you think they give you eternal life.
But the Scriptures point to me!
Yet you refuse to come to me to receive this life."
JOHN 5:39-40 NLT

Approaching Jesus can be intimidating. You may be afraid of what he might say. You might even hope that reading the Word and rushed prayers won't disrupt your life. But Jesus wants to shake up your routine and renew the parts that are lacking in vibrant life. Scripture is good because it begs you to intimately connect with your Savior.

Do you allow the Word of God to infuse every dimension of your life?

PHYSICAL TOUCH

"Take Joshua son of Nun, a man in whom is the spirit, and lay your hand on him. Give him some of your authority so the whole Israelite community will obey him."

NUMBERS 27:18, 20 NIV

Physical contact can affirm verbal communication. Moses is told by God to bring Joshua before the people and to lay his hand on him in order to show God's approval for the power shift. In 1 Timothy, Paul told Timothy that he received his gifts when the elders laid hands on him. You must recognize the need for both verbal and physical communication.

Are you able to use physical touch to advance the kingdom of God?

ADDING WORDS

Every word of God is flawless;
he is a shield to those who take refuge in him.
Do not add to his words,
or he will rebuke you and prove you a liar.
PROVERBS 30:5-6 NIV

When you believe the Bible is your protection, you must take great care in how you convey its truth. Let it speak for itself. It's not your job to make the listener agree. You can simply share what the Bible says and trust that God will water and grow his truth for his purposes.

Do you lean into the truth of God and its sufficiency?

LONG-TERM PLANS

Salmon begot Boaz, and Boaz begot Obed;
Obed begot Jesse, and Jesse begot David.
RUTH 4:21-22 NKJV

Naomi's search for a husband for Ruth resulted in the birth of Jesus Christ. Boaz didn't know this when Ruth became his wife. God, however, did. Long-term plans are why God told the Israelites to tell their children about his story. You don't know what God will do with you or your children, but you are a participant in his long-term plans when you are obedient today.

Are you available for God's long-term plans?

DOING GOOD

As for you, brothers, do not grow weary in doing good.
2 THESSALONIANS 3:13 ESV

Doing what is right and good may feel thankless and difficult, but it is always worth it. You might think that it doesn't matter or that nobody notices how hard you work to live the way God says you should live. Don't grow weary now. Nothing you give to God is fruitless. Every decision you make to do what is good gives God one more tool in his toolbox, and he is working to build something beautiful in your life.

Are you forging ahead on the path God has set for you?

PREPARATION

Remember your Creator in the days of your youth.
ECCLESIASTES 12:1 NIV

Life is a one-way journey, and you have your own unique path from which you cannot turn back. It's important to be wise! That is why Scripture instructs you to remember your Creator and to seek first his kingdom. How foolish would it be to not listen to God's wisdom? Take time to read the Word and learn God's principles that prepare you for life.

Have you sought God's wisdom and read the stories in his Word?

OBEDIENCE

"Do not eat or drink for three days, night or day.
My maids and I will do the same. And then, though it is against the law,
I will go in to see the king. If I must die, I must die."
ESTHER 4:16 NLT

God asks you for obedience, but he doesn't require specific results. Esther was unsure of what would come of her actions, but she was certain of what she needed to do. You can miss opportunities to serve God when you focus on the outcomes. Life with him is not about results; it is about obedience.

Are you prepared to be obedient to God regardless of the apparent outcome?

WELL DONE

"Well done, good and faithful servant! You have been faithful with a few things; I will put you in charge of many things. Come and share your master's happiness!"

MATTHEW 25:23 NIV

In the short twenty-four hours given to you each day, there is much to be done. You will sleep, eat, work, and spend time with family. How can you do each of these things and also glorify God and be faithful to him? God has put us in charge of just a few things. The way to join in the happiness of God is to be faithful in the few things he has given you.

Is it important to you that each item in your daily routine honors God?

GOD-BREATHED

All Scripture is God-breathed and is useful for teaching, rebuking, correcting and training in righteousness, so that the servant of God may be thoroughly equipped for every good work.

2 TIMOTHY 3:16-17 NIV

There's a mysterious weight to the actual, specific words in Scripture. If you forgo those words, you can alter the impact and truth of God's Word. It is worth quoting relevant verses at relevant times even though some people may respond with glazed eyes. The life God has breathed into his Word will come alive in the heart of the listener.

Have you memorized verses in the Bible that have had an impact on you?

STAND STRONG

Keep yourselves in God's love as you wait for the mercy of our Lord Jesus
Christ to bring you to eternal life.
JUDE 21 NIV

You are in the space between the resurrection and the return of Christ. During
this gap, it's important to show mercy, share with others, and hate evil. If you
work with someone who is anxious, be merciful, gracious, and kind. Is a friend
in danger? Act decisively. Does a family member need to be convicted of sin?
Share the character of God with them. God has placed people in your life for a
purpose. Know them and discern what they need.

Can you discern the needs of the people around you?

WITNESSES

We have all of these great witnesses who encircle us like clouds. So we must let go of every wound that has pierced us and the sin we so easily fall into. Then we will be able to run life's marathon race with passion and determination, for the path has been already marked out before us.
HEBREWS 12:1 TPT

Some people perform better when others are watching. They fight harder, strive further, and endure longer knowing people are paying attention. When you are not being observed, it's easier to succumb to the struggle. Through others, God cheers you on to be freed from anything that hinders your relationships.

Are you a good example to the people in your life who are watching you?

WHAT YOU WEAR

Since God chose you to be the holy people he loves, you must clothe yourselves with tenderhearted mercy, kindness, humility, gentleness, and patience.
COLOSSIANS 3:12 NLT

The kind of clothes a man wears isn't nearly as important as the condition of his heart. As a believer, you will find this is especially true because, whether you like it or not, a follower of Christ is a strategic representative of God. When you clothe yourself in mercy in the middle of trouble, choose patience over raising your voice in frustration, or consistently encourage those around you, people notice. They will trust God when they see him in you.

What spiritual clothes do you try to put on each day?

CONTENT

I know what it is to be in need, and I know what it is to have plenty.
I have learned the secret of being content in any and every situation,
whether well fed or hungry, whether living in plenty or in want.

PHILIPPIANS 4:12 NIV

You may think of contentment as the satisfaction of all your needs. If that were true, it would only be possible to be content if everything were perfect. God gives you the power and the peace to be okay even when everything around you is not perfect. True contentment comes from your relationship with him, not those pesky circumstances.

Does your level of contentment reside fully in your relationship with God?

DEVOTED TO PRAYER

Devote yourselves to prayer with an alert mind and a thankful heart.
COLOSSIANS 4:2 NLT

Stop and pray. Put aside your anxieties and have a conversation with God. What has he done lately in your life that makes you thankful? Do you need to realign yourself? Ask God what his plans are for you. Now pray for the people around you. What has God done for them that makes you thankful? What requests and needs do they have that you will entrust to the Lord? Ask God what he sees. Devote yourself to prayer.

Do you need a reminder to pray?

NEW NATURE

Put on your new nature, and be renewed
as you learn to know your Creator and become like him.
COLOSSIANS 3:10 NLT

God spoke and the stars were born. He said, "Let there be…" and it was. Christ was the Word who declared in the darkness that there should be light. Jesus speaks into your life today by declaring you to be free from sin. He calls you to him as he is calling you to change the world. His words beckon you to draw near as they empower you to move mountains. Be refreshed today. Put on the new nature given to you by Jesus, the Creator of the world.

Do you speak with Christ's voice, authority, and creativity?

EVERY OPPORTUNITY

Let your conversation be gracious and attractive
so that you will have the right response for everyone.
COLOSSIANS 4:6 NLT

Being a testimony to unbelievers is not about winning an argument. It's about living in a way that the circumstances of life cause them to notice you. You want people to see something different in you. When the moment comes and they ask, you'll be ready to share the source of your strength. It is in the everyday moments that your life has its greatest impact. How others see you in the routines, relationships, and messes of life is where God's gift in you is revealed.

Is God's redemptive love evident in the patterns of your daily living?

DON'T GET CAUGHT

Don't let anyone capture you with empty philosophies and high-sounding nonsense that come from human thinking and from the spiritual powers of this world, rather than from Christ.

COLOSSIANS 2:8 NLT

Satan captured Adam and Eve in the garden of Eden by hunting, luring, and ensnaring them. He tried again with Jesus in the desert. Every part of Satan's conversation was baited. But Jesus stayed the course and dispatched Satan's evil words by being even more shrewd. He overcame because he embodied uncompromising truth.

Are you armed with Christ's truth against empty philosophies and nonsense?

REPRESENTATIVE

We are Christ's ambassadors; God is making his appeal through us.
We speak for Christ when we plead, "Come back to God!"
2 CORINTHIANS 5:20 NLT

God is a good King who provides your daily bread, extends mercy to the troubled, and gives grace to his people. As you are Christ's representative, he entrusts you with his authority and his Words. When you speak, your words represent God's words. When you act, people watch for his grace and justice. Being Christ's ambassador gives you God's authority when you plead to those wandering to come back.

Are you honored to be an ambassador of Christ?

CONTINUE TO LIVE

Just as you accepted Christ Jesus as your Lord,
you must continue to follow him.
COLOSSIANS 2:6 NLT

To be a disciple of Christ means to be a lifelong learner. You follow Christ and spend time in the Word with more attention today than you did yesterday. Learn his thoughts, his actions, and his will. Seek his decisions, search his advice, and call for his wisdom. Run toward his healing, walk where he walks, and get into the mess whenever he puts himself there. If Jesus is your Lord, continue to follow him.

Are you resolved to stay the course?

BEING CONTENT

Not that I was ever in need,
for I have learned how to be content with whatever I have.
PHILIPPIANS 4:11 NLT

Paul never had it easy. He faced hardships and made mistakes, but his life changed dramatically when he met Jesus. Despite living sacrificially, Paul found contentment in Jesus. He learned that no matter his circumstances, he was grounded in who he was because of who Jesus was in his life. He found confidence in what he was called to do. Find your inner strength in the life of Jesus Christ today.

What helps you feel secure in who you are and what you're called to do?

WORK HARD

We tell others about Christ, warning everyone and teaching everyone with all the wisdom God has given us. That's why I work and struggle so hard, depending on Christ's mighty power that works within me.

COLOSSIANS 1:28-29 NLT

Paul tirelessly invested his life in the lives of others. His desire was to present people to God, perfected through the blood of Christ. He sought God's wisdom in practicing his faith so he would know how to represent God accurately. He worked hard, not for his own gain, but so others would discover and embrace the forgiveness and abundance that comes from knowing Jesus.

Are you using the strength of God to show Christ to those around you?

TRUSTING GOD TO SUPPLY

This same God who takes care of me will supply all your needs from his glorious riches, which have been given to us in Christ Jesus.
PHILIPPIANS 4:19 NLT

Do you have too much or are you lacking anything? Whether you have much or little, your life can be rich because of the presence of the people around you and your experiences today. Your responsibilities are a blessing from God. Your gifts are given to you so you can use them to bless others around you. God's grace is in your life, so you can calm your heart and extend your energy for his glory.

How might the Lord of all creation bless your heart, mind, soul, and strength?

CHANGING LIVES

This same Good News that came to you is going out all over the world.
It is bearing fruit everywhere by changing lives.
COLOSSIANS 1:6 NLT

God has called you specifically for his purposes. Embrace the good news and make the grace and truth of Jesus the central component of your life. Share the good news with those on your path. You know Jesus has truly impacted your life when he leads you to impact the lives of others. Your faith in God isn't actually yours; it is God's first, and yours to give away.

Do you wear your faith and bear fruit boldly?

PRIORITIES

All glory to God our Father forever and ever!
PHILIPPIANS 4:20 NLT

You may desire respect from your family, recognition from coworkers, and good standing within your community. Whatever causes you to seek approval from people, consider being proactive in seeking the Lord's approval first. The chief end of man is to bring glory to God. The honest question that you need to ask is who you want to see glorified in your life.

Where are you seeking validation?

BLESSINGS

May the grace of the Lord Jesus Christ be with your spirit.
PHILIPPIANS 4:23 NLT

You are in a privileged and unique situation to speak life into those who need your love. You have an opportunity to encourage those closest to you. God wants you to extend his blessings to others. Receive the grace God has for you through Jesus and be intentional about sharing it with others.

How do you reach out to others with the love of Jesus?